Language Arts
Grade 7

Copyright © 2014 by Houghton Mifflin Harcourt Publishing Company

Printed in the U.S.A.

ISBN   978-0-544-26790-9

4 5 6 7 8 9 10   2266   22 21 20 19 18 17

4500674434   B C D E F G

Core Skills Language Arts
GRADE 7
Table of Contents

Unit 5: Writing

Unit 6: Research Skills

Introduction

Core Skills Language Arts was developed to help your student improve the language skills he or she needs to succeed. The book emphasizes skills in the key areas of

- grammar
- punctuation
- vocabulary
- writing
- research

The more than 100 lessons included in the book provide many opportunities for your student to practice and apply important language and writing skills. These skills will help your student excel in all academic areas, increase his or her scores on standardized tests, and have a greater opportunity for success in his or her career.

About the Book

The book is divided into six units:

- Parts of Speech
- Sentences
- Mechanics
- Vocabulary and Usage
- Writing
- Research Skills

Your student can work through each unit of the book, or you can pinpoint areas for extra practice.

Lessons have specific instructions and examples and are designed for your student to complete independently. Grammar lessons range from using nouns and verbs to constructing better sentences. Writing exercises range from the how-to paragraph to the opinion essay. With this practice, your student will gain extra confidence as he or she works on daily school lessons or standardized tests.

A thorough answer key is also provided to check the quality of answers.

A Step Toward Success

Practice may not always make perfect, but it is certainly a step in the right direction. The activities in *Core Skills Language Arts* are an excellent way to ensure greater success for your student.

Unit 1: Parts of Speech
Common Nouns and Proper Nouns

A **noun** is a word that names a person, place, thing, or idea.

A **common noun** names any person, place, thing, or idea.
Examples: chemist, country, award

A **proper noun** names a particular person, place, thing, or idea. Notice that some proper nouns have more than one word.
Examples: Alfred Nobel, Sweden, Nobel Prize, Federalism

Underline the common nouns and circle the proper nouns in each sentence.

1. Uncle Harry enjoys mysteries more than other kinds of books.

2. He stayed up all night to finish *The Hound of the Baskervilles.*

3. This scary tale was written by Sir Arthur Conan Doyle.

4. Doyle created the famous, fictional character Sherlock Holmes.

5. Our whole class read the book *Encyclopedia Brown Carries On.*

Write a common noun to replace the proper noun. Then, write a sentence using the common noun.

6. Solitaire _____

_____

7. Sojourner Truth _____

_____

Write a proper noun to replace the common noun. Then, write a sentence using the proper noun.

8. singer _____

_____

9. country _____

_____

Collective Nouns and Mass Nouns

A **collective noun** is a common noun that names a group with more than one member.
Examples: jury, brigade, staff

A **mass noun** is a common noun that cannot be easily separated into countable units.
Examples: water, sand, wood, air, gold, cement

Underline the collective nouns in the sentences.

1. Flocks of penguins live only in the Southern Hemisphere.

2. Many scientific groups have studied the birds carefully.

3. A committee of biologists is studying the penguins living in New Zealand.

4. The scientists are developing a large collection of facts about the unusual birds.

5. They plan to give talks to science classes at the high school.

6. A large crowd is expected.

Write sentences using the collective nouns.

7. company _____

8. family _____

9. crowd _____

Underline the mass nouns in the sentences.

10. When you go to the store, don't forget the bread.

11. Get a large jar of grape jelly, too.

12. My best friend is allergic to the pollen from oak trees.

13. This fine yellow dust can cover sidewalks and fill gutters.

Write sentences using the mass nouns.

14. grass _____

15. oxygen _____

Pronouns

A **pronoun** is a word that takes the place of one or more than one noun. Pronouns show number and gender.

Number tells whether a pronoun is singular or plural.

Gender tells whether a pronoun is masculine, feminine, or neuter.

Examples:

Noun	Pronoun	Number and Gender
Bill McCoy heard	*He* heard	singular, masculine
a *librarian* tell	*her* tell	singular, feminine
stories.	*them.*	plural, neuter

Using pronouns helps writers avoid repeating the same noun over and over.

Write the pronoun from each sentence. Then, write the noun that each pronoun refers to.

1. When Marie Dorion went with the trappers to Oregon, they showed the young woman great respect.

   _____

2. Marie loved Pierre Dorion and agreed to travel with him to the wild new territory.

   _____

3. The couple had two sons, and they grew into big, strong boys.

   _____

4. One bitter winter brought a violent snowstorm, and it trapped the young family for 53 days.

   _____

5. Marie and Pierre promised the boys that they would survive.

   _____

Underline the pronouns in the sentences. Write the number and gender of each one.

6. Leon asked Anne to tell him about some of her favorite books. _____

7. Anne chose some books and opened them. _____

8. "Biographies about women pioneers are interesting. I could talk about one of them."_____

   _____

Subject, Object, and Possessive Pronouns

A **subject pronoun** acts as the subject of a sentence or as a predicate nominative.
Subject pronouns: *I, you, he, she, it, we, they*

Example: *The frightened mother* dialed 9-1-1. *She* dialed 9-1-1.

An **object pronoun** can be a direct object, an indirect object, or an object of a preposition.
Object pronouns: *me, you, him, her, it, us, them*

Example: The operator told *the woman* to stay calm. The operator told *her* to stay calm.

A **possessive pronoun** shows ownership. It takes the place of a possessive noun.
Possessive pronouns: *my, mine, your, yours, his, her, hers, its, our, ours, their, theirs*

Example: *Selena's* dream was to be a Latina diva. *Her* dream was to be a Latina diva.

Underline the pronoun in each sentence. Then, identify it by writing *subject*, *object*, or *possessive* on the line.

1. When Monica got caught in the storm, she was careful to drive slowly. _subject_____

2. Monica's younger brothers were with her. _object_____

3. Because of its icy surface, the highway was becoming dangerous. _possesive____

4. Monica drove slowly, but she still lost control. _subj._____

5. Bobby and Jerome got scared, and they started crying. _sub._____

6. When the children began to wail, Monica became impatient with them. _obj._____

7. "We must stay calm!" Monica ordered. _s_____

8. Her voice was shaking with tension. _pos._____

Write *subject*, *object*, or *possessive* to identify each pronoun. Then, use each pronoun correctly in a sentence.

9. I _____

_____

10. their _____

_____

11. him _____

_____

Demonstrative, Indefinite, Interrogative, and Reflexive Pronouns

Demonstrative pronouns point out particular persons, places, or things. The demonstrative pronouns are *this, these, that,* and *those.*

Example: *That* will be a difficult assignment.

Indefinite pronouns point out persons, places, or things, but less clearly than demonstrative pronouns do. Some common indefinite pronouns are *anything, no one, all, some,* and *several.*

Example: Not *everyone* will like the new rules.

An **interrogative pronoun** asks a question. The interrogative pronouns are *who, whom, whose, what,* and *which* when they are used to ask a question.

Example: *Who* put the dogs outside?

A **reflexive pronoun** ends in *self* or *selves.* Reflexive pronouns refer back to the subject of the sentence.

Example: My puppy entertains *himself* by chasing his tail.

Underline the pronoun in each sentence. Then, identify it by writing *demonstrative, interrogative, indefinite,* or *reflexive* on the line.

demonstrative   **1.** These are examples of Early American samplers.

reflexive   **2.** Olivia has educated herself about samplers.

Indefinite   **3.** Everyone comments on the beauty of the materials and colors.

Interrogative   **4.** Which does Olivia like best?

Indef.   **5.** Olivia likes everything in the collection.

Ind.   **6.** Study the samplers carefully because each portrays a specific theme.

Demonsh.   **7.** That was stitched by a seven-year-old named Hannah.

refl.   **8.** Did Hannah teach herself the stitches?

Int.   **9.** What was Hannah thinking about?

Ind.   **10.** No one knows for sure.

Action Verbs and Linking Verbs

> **Verbs** express action or being. An **action verb** expresses physical or mental action. It tells what the subject of a sentence does or did.
>
> *Example:*   The curtain to the great stage *opens* slowly.
>
> A **linking verb** expresses a state of being. It links the subject of a sentence with words that either describe the subject or rename it. The most common linking verb is *be*. Some forms of *be* are *am, is, are, was,* and *were*.
>
> *Examples:*   The stage sets *are* superb. The stage *is* a delight to the senses.
>
> Other common linking verbs are *seem, feel, appear, look, become, smell, taste,* and *grow*.
>
> *Examples:*   The audience *grows* quiet. They *seem* to be spellbound.

Underline the verb or verbs in each sentence. Then, write *action* or *linking* on the line.

1. In general, pigs struggle with a bad reputation. _____

2. To many people, pigs seem lazy, stupid, and dirty. _____

3. Pigs grunt and wallow in the mud all day, right? _____

4. Actually, pigs are very intelligent animals. _____

5. My best friend at school adores pigs. _____

6. He brought his piglet into homeroom one day. _____

7. While it cruised the classroom, the pig oinked loudly. _____

8. Then, it ate Amy Sutton's lunch—paper bag and all. _____

9. Afterwards, the pig looked surprised at the uproar. _____

10. Fortunately, Amy seemed OK with the loss of her lunch. _____

Write *action* or *linking* to identify each verb. Then, use the verb correctly in a sentence.

11. become _____

   _____

12. repair _____

   _____

Main Verbs and Helping Verbs

A **verb phrase** contains one **main verb** and one or more **helping verbs**.

A **main verb** expresses the action or state of being in the sentence.

Example: I have *read* some boring books lately.

A **helping verb** (auxiliary verb) helps the main verb express the action more precisely. The most common helping verbs are forms of *be, do,* and *have*. Other helping verbs include *can, may,* and *will*. A main verb can have more than one helping verb.

Examples: I *have* read some boring books lately.   They *have been* putting me to sleep.

Main verbs are always the last word of a verb phrase. Helping verbs always precede the main verb. Sometimes a verb phrase is interrupted by another part of speech.

Example: I will *never* finish the book at this rate.

Underline each verb phrase. Write the main and helping verbs on the lines.

1. You may know about the job of ghostwriter.

   main: _____   helping: _____

2. Ghostwriters do not haunt anyone.

   main: _____   helping: _____

3. They can help amateur writers with their manuscripts.

   main: _____   helping: _____

4. Ghostwriters have helped with some famous books.

   main: _____   helping: _____

5. You might not know the real writer of *The Personal Memoirs of Ulysses S. Grant.*

   main: _____   helping: _____

6. Grant had dictated his life story to a secretary.

   main: _____   helping: _____

Add a helping verb to each sentence below.

7. If I _____ find a ghostwriter, I might write a book myself.

8. I wonder how much a ghostwriter _____ charge.

Verb Tenses: Present, Past, and Future

The **tense** of a verb shows time. Verb tenses change to indicate that events happen at different times. The simple tenses are *present, past,* and *future.*

Present tense shows action that happens now or action that happens over and over. **Past tense** tells that something took place in the past. The action is over. **Future tense** tells that something will happen in the future. Add *will* to the main verb to form the future tense.

Examples: Jason *laughs* at Grandpa's silly story. Yesterday, he *laughed* for five minutes without a rest. Probably Jason *will laugh* at Grandpa's next story, too.

Underline the verb or verbs in each sentence. Then, write *present, past,* or *future* on the line.

1. My grandparents act in community theater productions. _present_

2. Tomorrow, they will practice for four hours. _future_

3. I always memorize their lines and test them. _pres._

4. Last night, they invited me to a rehearsal of their new play. _past_

5. Ruth Rosen created and will direct *The Lines Punched Back.* _fut._

6. The baseball league adds strong new teams every year. _pr._

7. Our team will face its biggest challenge today. _f._

8. The players field the ball well, but we lost the last game anyway. _pr past_

9. Mary pitched seven innings last time, and she will be our starting pitcher today. _past f._

10. Will the coach replace her during the game? _f. pr._

Write a sentence with each verb. Use the tense given in parentheses.

11. wander (past) _____

_____

12. explore (future) _____

_____

13. observe (present) _____

_____

14. indicate (future) _____

_____

Verb Tenses: Present Perfect, Past Perfect, and Future Perfect

The **perfect tense** of a verb shows the continuation or completion of an action. The three perfect tenses are *present perfect, past perfect,* and *future perfect.* To form the perfect tenses, use the past participle of the verb and a form of the helping verb *have.*

Present perfect tense shows action that started to happen sometime before now or action that is still happening.

Example: Mr. Lee *has started* the rehearsal already.

Past perfect tense shows action that happened before another past action.

Example: By third period, I *had planned* my entire act.

Future perfect tense shows action that will be completed before a stated time in the future.

Example: I *will have finished* my audition before class is over.

Complete each sentence. Use the main verb and the verb tense identified in parentheses.

1. (*paint*, present perfect) Believe it or not, the famous Pablo Picasso ___painted___ on paper bags.

2. (*develop*, past perfect) Before that, most paper bag art ___had developed___ from kindergarten projects.

3. (*exist*, present perfect) Brown paper bags ___existed___ for only 100 years.

4. (*achieve*, present perfect) Charles Stilwell ___achieved___ his place in history as the inventor of the brown paper bag.

5. (*carry*, past perfect) Before Stilwell's time, people ___had carried___ baskets when they shopped.

6. (*improve*, present perfect) Stilwell's invention, strong, stackable, and able to stand alone, ___improved___ shopping convenience significantly.

7. (*earn*, future perfect) With a revolutionary idea like Stilwell's, someday I ___will have earned___ a fortune!

8. (*start*, past perfect) If only I ___had started___ on it earlier.

Transitive Verbs and Intransitive Verbs

> A **transitive verb** is an action verb that is followed by a noun or pronoun. The noun or pronoun receives the action expressed in the verb and is called a *direct object*.
>
> *Examples:* During the Middle Ages, blacksmiths *repaired* tools and *forged* new weapons.
>
> **Intransitive verbs** include all linking verbs. Action verbs that do not have a direct object are also intransitive verbs.
>
> *Examples:* The cart of the hot dog vendor *was* in flames. (linking verb)
> The people *stopped* and *stared* at the fire. (action verbs without a direct object)

Underline the verbs in the sentences. Write *transitive* or *intransitive* on the line.

1. Greyfriars Bobby was a Skye terrier. _____

2. Bobby and his master, Auld Jock, lived in the hills outside Edinburgh. _____

3. The loyal animal loved Auld Jock intensely. _____

4. Auld Jock showed his dog great kindness. _____

5. One winter, Auld Jock suddenly died. _____

6. His friends gave him a funeral service in Greyfriars Churchyard. _____

7. Bobby was utterly grief-stricken. _____

8. The day after the service, the churchyard caretaker stopped and stared. _____

9. Greyfriars Bobby had found a home on top of Jock's grave. _____

10. Every day, an innkeeper and his wife brought food to the churchyard. _____

11. The people of Edinburgh told the story of Greyfriars Bobby. _____

12. Bobby gave a friendly wag of his tail to churchyard visitors. _____

Write two sentences for each verb. In the first sentence, use the verb as an intransitive verb. In the second sentence, use the verb as a transitive verb. Sentences may be written in any of the verb tenses you know: present, past, future, or any of the perfect tenses.

13. to surprise Intransitive: _____

   Transitive: _____

14. to tell Intransitive: _____

   Transitive: _____

The Principal Parts of Verbs

The four basic forms of a verb are its principal parts: the **present**, the **present participle**, the **past**, and the **past participle**.

A **participle** is the form a verb takes when it is combined with a helping verb such as *be* or *have*. For regular verbs, the **present participle** is formed by adding *ing* to the present.

Examples: disappear   (is, are, am) disappearing

For regular verbs, the **past** is formed by adding *ed* or *d* to the present. The **past participle** is formed when a helping verb such as *have* is added to the past.

Examples: disappeared   (has, have, had) disappeared

The four parts of a few verbs are shown below.

Present	Present Participle	Past	Past Participle
repeat	(is, are, am) repeating	repeated	(has, have, had) repeated
suggest	(is, are, am) suggesting	suggested	(has, have, had) suggested
continue	(is, are, am) continuing	continued	(has, have, had) continued
investigate	(is, are, am) investigating	investigated	(has, have, had) investigated

Write the correct form of the verb in parentheses.

1. (*jog*, present) Every year, runners _____ for miles in the New York Marathon.

2. (*race*, past participle) Drivers _____ sleek cars around the track at the Indianapolis 500 for years.

3. (*follow*, present participle) But in Alaska this March, the runners _____ along behind dog sleds.

4. (*extend*, present) The 1,000-mile course of the Iditarod Sled Dog Race _____ from Anchorage to Nome.

5. (*commemorate*, present) The Iditarod race _____ a real-life race against death.

6. (*start*, past participle) By the winter of 1925, the Alaskan Gold Rush _____ .

7. (*threaten*, past) Suddenly, an epidemic of diphtheria _____ Nome.

8. (*carry*, past) A relay of brave dog sledders _____ lifesaving serum from Anchorage to Nome.

9. (*try*, present participle) This year, dozens of dog sledders _____ to re-create the famous rescue.

Irregular Verbs

Form the past tense of regular verbs by adding *ed* or *d* to the end of the word. Form the past participle of a regular verb by adding *have, has,* or *had* to the past tense.

The past tense and past participle of an **irregular verb** do not end in *ed* or *d*. You must memorize the past tense and past participle of irregular verbs. Three parts of a few irregular verbs are shown below.

Present	Past	Past Participle
begin	began	(has, have, had) begun
forget	forgot	(has, have, had) forgotten
go	went	(has, have, had) gone
write	wrote	(has, have, had) written

Dictionaries include the past and past participle forms of irregular verbs.

Write the correct form of the verb in parentheses.

1. (take) Termites have _____ over our home.

2. (know) I wish I had _____ they made such lousy pets.

3. (get) Those termites have _____ some delicious wooden meals at my house.

4. (grow) Each disgusting bug has _____ to a shocking size.

5. (wear) Some even have _____ my husband's ties.

6. (ride) Yesterday, my youngest child _____ one around the porch.

7. (choose) Last winter, the termites _____ to eat the north wall.

8. (freeze) We almost _____ before the spring came.

Find the error or errors in each sentence. Write the sentence correctly.

9. Celia has came to the family reunion for five years. _____

_____

10. Her friend brung her this year because she had a broken arm. _____

_____

11. Paolo driven up to the entrance in a big black car. _____

_____

Adjectives

> **Adjectives** modify, or describe, nouns or pronouns. Adjectives tell *what kind, how many,* or *which one.*
>
> *Examples:*   The *gentle* purr of the *two* kittens was the *last* sound I heard.
>
> The adjectives *a, an,* and *the* are called **articles**. Use *a* before a word that begins with a consonant. Use *an* before a word that begins with a vowel or a vowel sound.
>
> *Examples:*   *A* kitten can develop into *a* cat with *an* attitude.
>
> A **proper adjective** is an adjective that is formed from a proper noun. A proper adjective always begins with a capital letter.
>
> *Examples:*   Albert Schweitzer was a *German* doctor who worked in *African* hospitals.
>
> Skilled writers use adjectives to make sentences more **vivid**.
>
> *Examples:*   The library has a collection of scrolls.
> The library has *an immense* collection of *ancient* scrolls.

Underline the adjectives in each sentence, except the articles (a, an, the). Then, write the nouns they modify.

1. The powerful lion is actually a sociable creature. _____

2. Mischievous cubs are taught important skills by watchful adults. _____

3. In ancient times, lions roamed the grassy areas of Europe and India. _____

4. Today, only a small number of lions survive in Asia. _____

Underline each adjective once. Underline each proper adjective twice. Circle each article.

5. A British guide accompanied us on a tour of the Mediterranean area.

6. Fortunately, the English language is spoken in most countries.

7. The African nations that border the sea are fascinating countries.

8. Seeing the Egyptian pyramids was an unforgettable experience.

Rewrite the sentence, adding vivid adjectives.

9. I saw a caterpillar munching a leaf in a tree. _____

_____

More About Adjectives

Demonstrative adjectives point out a noun. The words *this, that, these,* and *those* are demonstrative adjectives. Demonstrative adjectives are more precise than articles because they tell which one.

Examples: *This* book has more illustrations than *that* magazine.

Demonstrative adjectives always modify a noun. Demonstrative pronouns (page 5) replace a noun rather than modifying it.

Examples: *That* assignment will be difficult. (adjective)

That will be a difficult assignment. (pronoun)

Nouns, pronouns, and verbs can be used as adjectives because the way a word is used determines its part of speech.

Examples: *Our* family has always run a farm. Today, *family* farms have a hard time surviving.
Farming equipment is costly.

Underline the demonstrative adjectives and pronouns. Write *adjective* or *pronoun* on the line. Rewrite each sentence, changing demonstrative adjectives to pronouns and vice versa.

1. Those are my favorite books. _____

   _____

2. This collection of African instruments is magnificent. _____

   _____

3. These instruments are called *kalimbas*, or "thumb pianos." _____

   _____

4. This is a superior example of early African artistry. _____

   _____

Identify the part of speech of each underlined word. Circle *N* for noun, *P* for pronoun, *A* for adjective, or *V* for verb.

5. The <u>number</u> of large factory farms is increasing.	N	P	A	V
6. Factory farms <u>keep</u> hundreds of roosting chickens cooped up together.	N	P	A	V
7. The chickens are <u>debeaked</u>, and they are fed antibiotics.	N	P	A	V
8. <u>Bright</u> lights burn all day to encourage the hens to lay eggs.	N	P	A	V

Comparing with Adjectives

An adjective has three degrees of comparison: **positive, comparative,** and **superlative**.

A **positive adjective** is used when no comparison is being made.

Examples: How *old* the Inca empire seems! How *ancient* the Inca empire seems!

A **comparative adjective** is used to compare two items. Form the comparative of most one-syllable adjectives by adding *er.* For most adjectives with two or more syllables, add the word *more* before the adjective.

Examples: The Aztec empire is *older* than the Inca empire.
The Aztec empire is *more ancient* than the Inca empire.

A **superlative adjective** is used to compare three or more items. Form the superlative of most one-syllable adjectives by adding *est.* For most adjectives with two or more syllables, add the word *most* before the adjective.

Examples: The Mayan empire is the *oldest* one in the Americas.
The Mayan empire is the *most ancient* one in the Americas.

Some adjectives have special forms for comparing.

Examples: good, better, best

Write the correct form of the adjective in parentheses. Then, write *positive*, *comparative*, **or** *superlative* **to identify the degree of comparison.**

1. (strange) Which is _____, truth or fiction? _____

2. (reliable) Thousands of _____ witnesses have reported seeing aliens from outer

   space. _____

3. (weird) One of the _____ of all insects is the female praying mantis, which

   eats its mate alive. _____

4. (long) The tubes in just one of your kidneys are much _____ than your trip to

   camp—40 miles! _____

5. (amazing) Some would vote crystals the _____ things on Earth.

   _____

Adverbs

Adverbs modify a verb, an adjective, or another adverb. Adverbs tell *how, when, where, how often,* and *to what extent.* Many adverbs end in *ly.*

Examples: The joggers dressed *warmly* before they headed *outside.* (tell *how* and *where*)

Place adverbs that modify adjectives or other adverbs just before the word they modify.

Examples: The air was *quite* cold. The joggers hoped they would warm up *very* quickly.

Adverbs that modify verbs can be placed almost anywhere in the sentence.

Examples: *Suddenly,* the wind rose. The wind rose *suddenly.*

Negatives are words that mean "no," such as *not, never, nowhere, neither,* and *barely.* Negatives often function as adverbs.

Examples: I can *hardly* believe that you have *never* eaten oysters.

Underline each adverb and circle the word it modifies. Write whether the adverb tells *how, when, where, how often,* or *to what extent.*

1. You may firmly believe that the existence of UFOs is a hoax. _____

2. Many nonbelievers have completely changed their minds. _____

3. More and more strange, luminous craft are being sighted overhead. _____

4. Weather balloons and aircraft fool people sometimes. _____

5. Some people will never be convinced. _____

Circle the word that the underlined adverb modifies. Write *verb, adjective,* or *adverb* on the line.

6. The serious surfers arrive <u>first</u> on the beach. _____

7. They are <u>most</u> likely to be in the water by 5:30 A.M. _____

8. Lifeguards watch the swimmers <u>carefully</u>. _____

9. A strong undertow can be <u>very</u> dangerous. _____

10. Lifeguards shouted <u>very</u> loudly to those in the water. _____

11. Our lifeguard warned the swimmer <u>sternly</u>. _____

12. Some swimmers can be <u>rather</u> careless. _____

13. Smart swimmers <u>always</u> observe the rules. _____

Name _____ Date _____

Comparing with Adverbs

Adverbs can be used to compare two or more actions. A **positive adverb** is used when no comparison is being made.

Examples: I studied *hard* for the test. Snow falls *frequently* in Vermont.

A **comparative adverb** is used to compare two actions. Form the comparative by adding *er* to the positive form or by placing the word *more* or *less* before the adverb.

Examples: I must study *harder* this year than last year. Snow comes *more frequently* when the wind is from the north.

A **superlative adverb** compares three or more actions. Form the superlative by adding *est* to the positive form or by placing the word *most* or *least* before the adverb.

Examples: I will study *hardest* for final exams. Snow comes *most frequently* during February.

Some adverbs have special forms for comparing.

Examples: badly, worse, worst

The underlined words are adverbs. Write *positive, comparative,* or *superlative* to identify the degree of comparison.

1. Rainstorms <u>commonly</u> occur in cities like Seattle that are close to the ocean. _____

2. In which areas of the world are rainstorms <u>most likely</u> to occur? _____

3. Scientists tell us that rainstorms occur <u>more frequently</u> in tropical climates than in temperate zones.

_____

4. It seems to rain <u>constantly</u> in the forests of Central America. _____

5. Clouds fill with moisture <u>more readily</u> over water than over land. _____

6. If you don't like rainstorms, it is <u>better</u> to live inland than on the coast. _____

7. The <u>worst</u> place of all for severe weather would be an island in the South Pacific. _____

Write your own adverb to complete each sentence. Use the degree of comparison indicated in parentheses.

8. (positive) Karli yearns _____ to go to high school.

9. (comparative) Her brother, who is a junior, does _____ than Karli on report cards.

10. (comparative) Karli is _____ interested in football games than report cards.

Name _____ Date _____

Adverb or Adjective?

Adverbs modify verbs, adjectives, or other adverbs. Adjectives modify nouns and pronouns.

Examples: We may never know the *real* facts in the case. (adjective)

We may never *really* know the facts in the case. (adverb)

The words *good* and *well* are often confused. *Good* is an adjective and, therefore, always modifies a noun or pronoun.

Example: A *good* book and a rainy day are a great combination.

Well is usually an adverb used to tell how something is done. *Well* is an adjective only when it means "healthy."

Examples: Jesse felt *well* after the surgery. (adjective)

The surgery went *well*. (adverb)

**Write the word in parentheses that completes each sentence correctly.
Write *adjective* or *adverb* on the line.**

1. (strange, strangely) Some _____ stones stand in Salisbury, England.

   _____

2. (strange, strangely) From a distance, they seem to hang _____ in the air.

   _____

3. (unusual, unusually) They are the _____ Standing Stones of Stonehenge.

   _____

4. (unusual, unusually) Their mystery has been _____ difficult to solve.

   _____

5. (immense, immensely) Many of the stones are _____. _____

6. (immense, immensely) Scientists find it _____ difficult to explain how they

   got there. _____

7. (good, well) The passing years have hidden Stonehenge's purpose _____.

   _____

8. (good, well) The mystery of Stonehenge would be a _____ subject for a report.

   _____

Name _____ Date _____

Prepositions and Prepositional Phrases

> A **preposition** shows the relationship of a noun or pronoun to some other word or words in a sentence. Common prepositions include *about, with, in, for, to,* and *of.*
>
> *Example:* The average four-year-old asks 437 questions *during* a single day.
>
> An **object of a preposition** is the noun or pronoun that follows a preposition.
>
> *Example:* The average four-year-old asks 437 questions during a single *day.*
>
> A **prepositional phrase** is made up of a preposition, the object of the preposition, and all the words in between.
>
> *Example:* The average four-year-old asks 437 questions *during a single day.*

The underlined word in each sentence is the object of the proposition. Write the preposition for each object on the line.

1. The rudder, the single mast, and the compass were all invented by the <u>Chinese</u>. _____

2. Can you imagine steering a boat without a <u>rudder</u>? _____

3. The compass made navigation through foggy and dark <u>nights</u> possible. _____

4. The compass was first mentioned in a <u>book</u> dated 1117. _____

5. The compass was actually invented at a much earlier <u>date</u>. _____

These sentences contain two prepositional phrases. Underline the first phrase, and circle the second one.

6. The average elevator in an office building travels about 10,000 miles during one year.

7. Some students believe that lying down with pillows under their feet helps them solve math problems.

8. The average American drinks about 28,000 quarts of milk in a lifetime.

9. Many passengers leaned over the railings of the large ship.

10. Visitors began to walk down the gangplank and onto the dock.

11. The ship would soon be sailing beneath an overcast sky into the cold Atlantic Ocean.

12. The young girl stood silently among the strangers and thought about her new life.

Prepositional Phrases Used as Adjectives and Adverbs

A prepositional phrase that modifies a noun or pronoun is functioning as an **adjective phrase**. Remember that adjectives tell *what kind, how many,* or *which one*.

A prepositional phrase that modifies a verb, an adjective, or another adverb is functioning as an **adverb phrase**. Remember that adverbs tell *how, when, where, how often,* and *to what extent*.

Examples: The whale *with the unusual markings* is our favorite.

(adjective phrase; tells which whale)

The tourists filmed the whales *with their video cameras*.

(adverb phrase; tells how)

Underline the adjective phrase in each sentence. Write the word it modifies.

1. Horseshoe crabs resemble hard hats with long tails. _____

2. They are close relatives of spiders. _____

3. The mouth of the horseshoe crab is well hidden. _____

4. It is an opening underneath the crab's body. _____

Underline the adverb phrase in each sentence. Write the word(s) it modifies.

5. Whales are the largest mammals that live on Earth. _____

6. Whales behave with great intelligence. _____

7. A whale must breathe air through its lungs. _____

8. Whales can dive for long periods. _____

Underline each prepositional phrase. Then, circle *ADJ* for adjective phrase or *ADV* for adverb phrase.

9. One rock sample from the moon is 4,720 million years old.	ADJ ADV
10. The rock was collected by the Apollo space mission.	ADJ ADV
11. The daytime temperature on the lunar equator is 243°F.	ADJ ADV
12. A black hole is formed by a star's complete collapse.	ADJ ADV
13. About 150 meteorites from space pound Earth each year.	ADJ ADV
14. An Alaskan, Mrs. E. H. Hodges, was hurt by a falling meteorite.	ADJ ADV

20

Conjunctions

Conjunctions connect words or word groups. The **coordinating conjunctions** *and, but,* and *or* join ideas that are similar. The **correlative conjunctions** (*either/or, neither/nor,* and *both/and*) join pairs of ideas.

Examples: Carelessness is the cause of many *falls and burns*.

The athletes will need *both skill and endurance* to win the playoffs.

The coordinating conjunctions *and, but, or, nor, for, so,* and *yet* are used to combine two sentences that are related. Remember to place a comma before the conjunction when you write sentences this way.

Example: Craig gets into trouble, *but* he usually gets out of it.

Underline each conjunction. Write *coordinating* or *correlative* on the line.

1. Neither Antonio nor I have ever seen a carnivorous plant. _____

2. Today, we went walking in the woods behind my house and saw something unusual. _____

3. We thought it was a pitcher plant, but we weren't sure. _____

4. Back at home, we researched pitcher plants and learned more about them. _____

5. Most pitcher plants live in bogs or wetlands. _____

6. The soil there has plenty of water but very few nutrients. _____

7. The pitcher plants must either obtain more nutrients or die. _____

8. They get their meals by trapping moths, wasps, and other bugs. _____

Combine the two sentences using a coordinating conjunction. Remember to punctuate the new sentence correctly.

9. Llamas are quite affectionate. They enjoy humans as company. _____

_____

10. Llamas have no natural defenses like horns. They spit to show they are mad. _____

_____

11. Llamas are tamer than farm animals. They make good pets. _____

_____

12. You can check out a book about llamas. You can research them on the Internet. _____

_____

More About Conjunctions

Subordinating conjunctions connect an independent clause with one or more dependent clauses. Some common subordinating conjunctions are *since, before,* and *unless.*

Example: *Because* dimples were in fashion in 1896, Martin Goetz invented a dimple-making machine.

Sometimes adverbs, such as *however*, are used as conjunctions. They are used to connect two independent clauses to form a compound sentence.

Example: Rainy weather is common in Seattle; *however*, most people don't mind it.

Write the subordinating conjunction on the line.

1. If you go to New York City, consider a visit to Brooklyn. _____

2. Fifteen teenagers there gained some fame because they were pollution fighters. _____

3. They called themselves the Toxic Avengers since that is the name of a pollution-fighting

   superhero. _____

4. Although it was located next to a school, the Radiac Research Corporation was storing large

   amounts of medical waste. _____

5. When the Toxic Avengers learned about this, they planned a rally. _____

6. Public awareness grew after the rally was held. _____

Connect the two sentences with an adverb from the box below. Write the new sentence on the line.

consequently	still	further	thus	however	because

7. Frank agreed to paint several rooms. He needed the money. _____

   _____

8. He knew the work would be dirty and exhausting. The price was right. _____

   _____

9. Frank scrubbed hard for two hours. The walls were free of dirt. _____

   _____

10. The paint on one wall was thin. He never would have noticed something beneath the surface.

   _____

Interjections

An **interjection** is a word or group of words that expresses emotion. Place an exclamation point following the interjection if it is used to express strong emotion. Express milder emotions by placing a comma between the interjection and the rest of the sentence.

Examples: *Well*, someone left the door open again.
Rats! I hope the dog didn't get out!

Add the correct punctuation to these sentences with interjections. Underline any words that should be capitalized.

1. Say you're not superstitious, are you?

2. Really no one believes in that silly stuff anymore.

3. Ouch I broke a mirror and cut my finger.

4. Oh no some people believe that's seven years' bad luck.

5. Hey we thought you didn't believe in superstitions.

6. Oops well it doesn't hurt to be careful.

Add an interjection to each sentence.

7. _____! Harry certainly is superstitious!

8. _____, I never knew that.

9. _____, he has more superstitions than anyone I know.

10. _____, did you know Harry believes that running around his house three times will improve his luck?

11. _____! He never gets out of bed on the left side because it's very bad luck.

12. _____, he also thinks wearing clothes wrong side out brings good luck.

Write sentences using the following interjections: *bravo, shh,* and *awesome.*

13. _____

14. _____

15. _____

Infinitives and Infinitive Phrases

An **infinitive** is a verb that functions as a noun, an adjective, or an adverb. The word *to* precedes the verb in an infinitive.

Example: Someday, I would like *to write* beautiful poetry.

An **infinitive phrase** includes an infinitive and its modifiers. It may also include an object of the infinitive and any modifiers of the object.

Examples: Someday, I would like *to write beautiful poetry.*

Readers sometimes confuse infinitives with prepositional phrases that begin with *to.* Remember that a verb follows *to* in an infinitive phrase. A noun or pronoun follows *to* in a prepositional phrase.

Underline the infinitive phrase in each sentence.

1. I like to work in my garden.

2. Each spring I wait impatiently to plant my garden.

3. I select special flowers to attract hummingbirds.

4. Perennials are the flowers I choose to grow here.

The underlined words are parts of infinitive phrases. Write *infinitive, object,* or *modifier* on the line.

5. You don't have to plant perennials every year, as you do annuals. _____object_____

6. Gardeners need to think about the time each perennial will bloom. _____infinitive_____

7. I don't need to tell you how satisfying a beautiful garden can be. _____obj._____

8. To have a beautiful garden, you must plan, dig, weed, and rearrange constantly. _____modifier_____

Expand the infinitives by adding an object or modifier or both. Then, write a sentence using the expanded phrase.

9. to encourage   expanded phrase: _____

   Sentence: _____

10. to protest   expanded phrase: _____

    Sentence: _____

11. to conceal   expanded phrase: _____

    Sentence: _____

Gerunds and Gerund Phrases

A **gerund** is a verb that ends in *ing* and functions as a noun.

Example: *Estimating* is an important mathematics skill.

A **gerund phrase** includes a gerund and its modifiers. It may also include an object of the gerund, and any modifiers of the object.

Example: *Writing a famous bestseller* is the goal of every novelist.

Because gerunds function as nouns, they have many uses. Gerunds can be the subject of a sentence, a direct object, or the object of a preposition.

Underline the gerund phrase in each sentence.

1. Running long distances is no problem for me.

2. My goal is jogging about three miles per day.

3. Giving in to aches and pains is not an option.

4. As they run along, some people enjoy reciting a favorite poem.

5. Refusing to quit is a characteristic of good runners.

The underlined words are parts of gerund phrases. Write *gerund*, *object*, or *modifier* on the line.

6. I like jogging along the seashore best. _gerund_

7. Breathing deeply is easier out in the fresh air. _modifier_

8. Feeling the crisp wind on my face is a unique experience. _modifier_

9. Sometimes, I use humming a tune as a way to keep going. _gerund_

10. Running a marathon next year is my New Year's resolution. _obj._

Write *subject*, *direct object*, or *object of preposition* to identify how the underlined gerund functions in each sentence.

11. Disciplining myself to run every day isn't as difficult as I thought. _subject_

12. I just concentrate on winning the Austin Marathon. _object of preposition_

13. I like looking around at the world as I run. _direct object_

14. As a matter of fact, other ways of exercising seem dull to me. _object of prep._

15. Achieving a goal is the best incentive for hard work. _s_

Participles and Participial Phrases

A **participle** is a verb that functions as an adjective. Both the present and past participle forms of the verb can be used as adjectives.

Examples: A *running* horse galloped down the road. *Dried* leaves flew from his hooves.

A **participial phrase** includes a participle and its modifiers. It may also include an object of the participle and any modifiers of the object.

Example: The child, *flashing a mischievous smile*, turned and walked away.

Underline the participial phrase in each sentence. Write the noun or pronoun it modifies on the line.

1. Living in the mountains, Josh learned to love nature. *Josh*

2. Josh could see birds perched on tree limbs. *birds*

3. He watched chipmunks scampering around briskly. *chipmunks*

4. His field guide, worn from use, helped him identify wildflowers. *guide*

The underlined words are participles or parts of participial phrases. Write *participle, object,* or *modifier* on the line.

5. People interested in soccer say he was the greatest player ever. *modifier*

6. A record-breaking crowd attended his final game in 1971. *participle*

7. The determined boy joined a professional team at age 15. *partic.*

8. The fans encircling the field were thrilled by his speed. *obj.*

Create the kind of participle indicated in parentheses. Expand it by adding an object, modifier, or both and write the phrase on the line. Then, write a sentence using the expanded phrase.

9. protect (present participle) expanded phrase: _____

   Sentence: _____

10. write (past participle) expanded phrase: _____

   Sentence: _____

Name _____ Date _____

Unit 2: Sentences
Simple Sentences and Word Order

> A **sentence** expresses a complete thought. At a minimum, it must contain a subject and a verb. **Simple sentences** contain only one complete thought.
>
> Most sentences use **natural word order**. The subject of the sentence comes first, followed by the verb and any objects. Some sentences, such as questions, have **inverted word order**. The verb, or part of it, comes first, followed by the subject.
>
> *Examples:*   The reptile Plateosaurus was 25 feet long. (natural word order)
>
> Do you think that is an exaggeration? (inverted word order)

Write *complete* or *incomplete* after each group of words to indicate whether the words express a complete thought.

1. Have you seen the Meteor Crater in Arizona? _____

2. About 4,150 feet across and about 570 feet deep. _____

3. A meteorite crashed there 50,000 years ago. _____

4. May have fallen even earlier. _____

5. In 1908, a meteorite streaked across the Siberian sky. _____

6. People could see it for hundreds of miles. _____

7. Really weigh hundreds of tons? _____

Rewrite each incomplete thought, or sentence fragment, you identified above to make it a sentence. Be sure each sentence expresses a complete thought and is punctuated correctly.

8. _____

9. _____

10. _____

Write *natural* or *inverted* to indicate the word order in each sentence.

11. High heels were first worn by men in the 1500s. _____

12. Do you know how high heels were first used? _____

13. They helped keep riders' feet in their stirrups. _____

14. Don't you assume that all footwear should include a right foot and a left foot? _____

15. Well, shoes in Colonial America were all made to fit either foot. _____

Types of Sentences

A **declarative sentence** makes a statement. Place a period at the end of a declarative sentence.

An **interrogative sentence** asks a question. Place a question mark at the end of an interrogative sentence.

An **imperative sentence** gives a command or makes a request. Place a period at the end of an imperative sentence.

An **exclamatory sentence** expresses strong feeling. Place an exclamation point at the end of an exclamatory sentence.

Examples: Janelle is painting a picture of an imaginary place. (*declarative* sentence)

Who could ever create a more imaginative scene? (*interrogative* sentence)

Plan to see her work as soon as you can. (*imperative* sentence)

What fantastic colors she uses! (*exclamatory* sentence)

Put the correct punctuation mark at the end of each sentence. Then, write *declarative, interrogative, imperative,* or *exclamatory* on the line.

1. Look carefully at that photograph _____

2. How did the photographer manage to capture such an unusual shot _____

3. What an interesting background the photo has _____

4. Photographers study for years to learn to use backgrounds effectively _____

5. What skill these artists possess _____

6. Observe the shape of the object in the picture _____

7. What do you think it could possibly be _____

8. Shots like this one create an eerie sense of emptiness _____

Rewrite each sentence as the kind of sentence identified in parentheses.

9. A llama is not a wild animal. (interrogative) _____

10. You might find it interesting to research the various habitats of the llama. (imperative) _____

_____

11. Don't llamas have only two toes on each foot? (declarative) _____

_____

Complete, Simple, and Compound Subjects

The **complete subject** of a sentence includes all the words that tell who or what the sentence is about.

Example: *Everyone in my house* is keeping a secret.

The **simple subject** is the main word or words in the complete subject.

Example: *Everyone* in my house is keeping a secret.

Sometimes the complete subject and the simple subject are the same.

Example: *Marlon* practiced and daydreamed for weeks before the game.

A **compound subject** contains two or more subjects that have the same verb. The simple subjects in a compound subject are usually joined by *and* or *or*.

Example: The *craters* and *plains* of the moon have had no human visitors for some time.

Underline the complete subject in each sentence. Then, write the simple subject on the line.

1. A wooden feeder for the birds hangs outside my window. _____

2. The clear, pleasant whistles of the goldfinches often echo in the trees nearby. _____

3. Our chubby orange kitty watches the birds from the window. _____

4. She can't figure out exactly what to do. _____

5. I feel sorry for our poor, confused feline. _____

6. *Birds of North America* helps us identify our feathered visitors. _____

7. A strong telescope can help bird-watchers see the birds from a far distance. _____

8. Even relatively small binoculars can help watchers recognize different species. _____

Underline the complete compound subject in each sentence. Circle the verb.

9. Myon and I went on a camping trip last fall.

10. Myon and his dad took charge of packing and finding a campground.

11. Myon, his dad, or I should have thought about planning for rain.

12. We and all our equipment were soaked through in the first ten minutes.

13. Our sleeping bags and down jackets looked like wet dishcloths.

14. Myon and I were wet, tired, and disappointed.

Name _____ Date _____

Complete, Simple, and Compound Predicates

The **complete predicate** of a sentence includes all the words that tell what the subject does or is.

Example: My two older brothers *stared at me silently.*

The **simple predicate** is the main verb in the complete predicate.

Example: My two older brothers *stared* at me silently.

A **compound predicate** contains two or more predicates that have the same subject. The simple predicates in a compound predicate are usually joined by *and, but,* or *or.*

Example: We *will find* the card catalog or *will ask* the librarian for help.

Underline the complete predicate in each sentence. Then, write the simple predicate on the line.

1. Ralph's father put the new plants on the ground. _____

2. The two gardeners dug a separate hole for each plant. _____

3. Ralph's sister Liz watered the plants generously. _____

4. Green leaves sprouted soon on all the plants. _____

5. All of the garden's plants were growing well. _____

6. None of the plants had bloomed, though. _____

7. Ralph and Liz inspected the garden one morning. _____

8. The smallest plant of all had suddenly produced three lovely flowers! _____

Underline the complete compound predicate in each sentence. Circle the simple subject.

9. Alfio Carlucci came out of the house and sat on the porch.

10. He enjoyed life on the farm but was a little lonely.

11. Alfio's friends lived several miles away and rarely visited.

12. Alfio's parents had immigrated to the United States in 2008 and settled on this remote farm.

13. They had worked hard to learn English but were still embarrassed about their accents.

14. Alfio longed for his own car and daydreamed of ways to pay for it.

15. The Carluccis talked with each other in the kitchen but kept their voices soft.

16. They knew of Alfio's loneliness and planned to do something about it.

Name _____ Date _____

Predicate Nominatives

A **predicate nominative** is a noun or pronoun that follows a linking verb and renames the subject.

Examples: Susan B. Anthony was an early *feminist*. (noun)

It was *she* who led the women's suffrage movement to victory. (pronoun)

Predicate nominatives sometimes contain more than one noun. These are called **compound predicate nominatives**.

Example: Mahatma Gandhi was a Hindu religious *leader* and a social *reformer* in India.

Write the predicate nominative from each sentence on the line. Some sentences have a compound predicate nominative.

1. Finland is a country with a language very different from English. _country_

2. Finnish citizens, though, are people just like us. _people_

3. Recently, I have become a pen pal to one of them. _pen pal_

4. Eric Hirvonen is a guy about my age. _guy_

5. He is a student and the son of a college professor. _student + son_

6. The capital city of Helsinki has been his home throughout his life. _home_

7. Although we are on opposite sides of the world, Eric and I are good friends. _friends_

8. Becoming a composer is my career choice. _choice_

9. Eric's goals are dancing and choreography. _dancing choreography_

10. Will Eric and I be friends for life? _friends_

11. I am not the one to decide that question. _one_

12. However, people can be friends for a long time. _friends_

13. Eric is a person I enjoy knowing. _person_

14. We hope to be visitors in each other's countries. _visitors_

15. Our visits would be happy experiences. _experiences_

16. Such experiences are memories we would enjoy. _memories_

Predicate Adjectives

A **predicate adjective** is an adjective that follows a linking verb and modifies the subject of a sentence.

Example: A freshly baked pie is *delightful* to the eye and nose.

Predicate adjectives sometimes contain more than one adjective. These are called **compound predicate adjectives**.

Example: The job applicant seems *honest* and *reliable*.

Write the predicate adjective from each sentence on the line. Some sentences may have a compound predicate adjective.

1. Columbus must have been aghast as he sailed near Bermuda. _____aghast_____

2. Suddenly, the sea was alive with vegetation. _____alive_____

3. The Sargasso Sea is totally eerie, even for a courageous explorer. _____eerie_____

4. The Sargasso is different from any other place on Earth. _____different_____

5. The sea looks solid from a distance. _____solid_____

6. It is strange to see a body of water so choked with seaweed. _____strange_____

7. The Sargasso is more saline and more barren than any other area in our oceans.

    _____saline barren_____

8. With its floating weeds, the sea is unique and therefore fascinating to scientists.

    _____unique fascinating_____

9. Sailors have always been fearful of the Sargasso. _____fearful_____

Write two sentences with each verb. In the first sentence, use the verb as an action verb. In the second sentence, use it as a linking verb with a predicate adjective.

10. taste _____

    _____

11. remain _____

    _____

12. grow _____

    _____

Direct Objects

A **direct object** is a noun or pronoun that follows an action verb. Direct objects tell *who* or *what* receives the action.

Examples: I inherited a pet *deer* from the former residents of my house. (tells *what*)

The surgical team asked *Dr. Habib* about the procedure. (tells *who*)

Underline the verb in each sentence. Then, write the direct object or objects on the line.

1. My dad <u>earns</u> money catching lobsters. _____ *money* _____

2. He <u>boards</u> his boat every day at dawn. _____ *boat* _____

3. The seagulls overhead <u>screech</u> a greeting. _____ *greeting* _____

4. From about a mile offshore, Dad <u>scans</u> the horizon. _____ *horizon* _____

5. Brightly colored buoys <u>mark</u> the positions of lobster traps. _____ *positions* _____

6. He <u>uses</u> white paint and orange flags on his buoys. _____ *paint flags* _____

7. With a winch, Dad <u>pulls</u> his traps up from the ocean floor. _____ *traps* _____

8. Inside, lobsters <u>wave</u> their pincer-like claws back and forth. _____ *claws* _____

9. Dad <u>slips</u> small wooden pegs in the claws' joints to keep them closed. _ *pegs* _

10. Soon, he <u>drops</u> the traps and the buoys back over the side of the boat. _ *traps buoys* _

11. My grandfather <u>cooks</u> the lobsters to perfection. _____ *lobsters* _____

12. He <u>memorized</u> the secret family recipe long ago. _____ *recipe* _____

Write two sentences with each verb. In the first sentence, include a direct object that tells *what*. In the second sentence, include a direct object that tells *who*. You may use any verb tense.

13. imagine _____

_____

14. find _____

_____

15. expect _____

_____

Indirect Objects

An **indirect object** is a noun or pronoun that follows an action verb. Indirect objects tell *to whom* or *for whom* the action of the verb is done.

For a sentence to have an indirect object, it must first have a direct object.

An indirect object is usually placed between the action verb and the direct object.

Examples: The vet sent *me* a reminder to bring my dogs in for their shots.

Before we left, I gave *each dog* a warning about politeness.

Underline the verb in each sentence. Write the direct object on the first line and the indirect object on the second.

1. My parents promised me riding lessons at the local stable.

   _____   _____

2. My awkward attempts only won me a horse laugh from the riding mistress.

   _____   _____

3. This dictionary of horse lore offers readers some interesting trivia about horses.

   _____   _____

4. For example, a wooden horse gave the people of Troy quite a surprise.

   _____   _____

5. And many years ago, Britons fed horses chestnuts as medicine.

   _____   _____

6. Our teacher told the class the story of the mythical horse Pegasus.

   _____   _____

7. In many fables, wise horses give their foolish masters important warnings.

   _____   _____

Write one sentence with each verb. Include a direct and indirect object in each one. You may use any verb tense.

8. bring _____

9. buy _____

10. hand _____

Appositives

An **appositive** is a noun that identifies or explains the noun or pronoun it follows.

Example: Nguyen Luong, the *judge*, sentenced the criminal to prison.

An **appositive phrase** consists of an appositive and its modifiers.

Example: Nguyen Luong, *the presiding judge of the high court*, sentenced the criminal to prison.

Appositives are usually set off in commas, although sometimes dashes are used.

Use commas to set off appositives that are not essential to the meaning of the sentence. Don't use commas to set off appositives when they are essential to understanding the nouns they explain.

Examples: The prairie, a kind of grassland, is home to many plants and animals.

Of all my relatives, my brother Boris is the weirdest.

Underline each appositive, and insert commas where they are needed.

1. The first wedding in America the marriage of Anne Burras and John Laydon took place in 1609.

2. The first wedding broadcast on radio took place at a fair the Electrical Exposition in 1922.

3. The wedding march was played by radio station KDKA in Pittsburgh a city seven miles away.

4. My favorite strange wedding a parachute ceremony took place in 1940.

5. The participants—a minister, a bride, a groom, and four musicians—were suspended from parachutes during the ceremony.

6. John Tyler the tenth president was the first to be married while he was president.

7. His first wife Letitia had died while he held that office.

8. A "balloon wedding" a ceremony in a hot-air balloon was held in 1874 in Ohio.

9. The city of Houston site of an air show was the location of the first wedding in an airplane.

Add an appositive to each sentence. Use commas if they are needed.

10. The scorpion has a poisonous sting. _____

_____

11. Researching the subject required many hours at the library. _____

_____

Phrases and Clauses

A **phrase** is a group of words that work together. A phrase does not have a subject or predicate. A phrase can be a prepositional, infinitive, gerund, or participial phrase.

Examples: *Running long distances* is no problem for me. (gerund phrase)

The mystery *of Stonehenge* is a good topic *for a report*. (prepositional phrases)

That man *kicking the soccer ball* is Pele. (participial phrase)

Someday, I would like *to write beautiful poetry*. (infinitive phrase)

A **clause** is a group of words that has a subject and a predicate.

Example: The senators left the capitol *after the session was adjourned*.

Identify each underlined group of words as a *phrase* or *clause*.

1. Oprah Winfrey was born on January 29, 1954, in Kosciusko, Mississippi. *phrase*

2. When she was seven years old, she moved to Nashville, Tennessee. *clause*

3. Her father encouraged her to read five books every two weeks. *phrase*

4. She became the first African American woman to host a nationally distributed weekday talk show on television. *phrase*

5. Her program, based in Chicago, went national in 1986. *phrase*

6. Besides having a successful television career, Oprah has starred as a film actor. *phrase*

7. She appeared in *The Color Purple* in 1985. *phrase*

8. As you know, this film was based on a novel by Alice Walker. *clause*

Each underlined group of words is a phrase. Write *prepositional, infinitive, gerund*, or *participial* to identify each phrase.

9. To have a beautiful garden, you must plant, dig, weed, and rearrange constantly. *infinitive*

10. Writing a best seller is the goal of every novelist. *gerund*

11. I like jogging along the seashore best. *prepositional*

12. Pele's first soccer ball was a stocking stuffed with rags. *participial*

13. Can you imagine steering a boat without a rudder? *prepost.*

14. The young musician's dream was to play in a famous symphony. *infin.*

Independent and Dependent Clauses

A **clause** is a group of words that has a subject and a predicate.

Examples: Indonesia includes more than 13,600 islands.

When Indonesia won its independence

An **independent clause** has a subject and predicate. It can stand alone as a sentence.

Example: Indonesia includes more than 13,600 islands.

A **dependent clause** has a subject and predicate, but it does not express a complete thought. Therefore, it cannot stand alone as a sentence.

Example: When Indonesia won its independence

A **subordinating conjunction** such as *until, when,* or *because* is often used to join a dependent clause and an independent clause.

Write the subject and the verb from each clause. Then, write *dependent* or *independent* on the line.

1. after the paint had been scraped away   paint   had been scraped   d

2. fill a bucket with washing compound   you   i

3. all day they continued to scrub   they

4. until shoulders and backs ached   d

5. before the painting was revealed   d

6. all the work was over   i

Write *dependent* or *independent* to identify the underlined clause. If the clause is dependent, write the subordinating conjunction that connects it with the rest of the sentence.

7. Diego Rivera was one of the greatest painters and muralists of Mexico.

_____ i _____

8. Because he loved Mexico, his works often portray the culture and history of that country.

_____ d _____

9. One of his paintings reflects the time before the Spanish conquered Mexico.

_____ d _____

10. That painting shows the Zapotec Indians making gold jewelry.

_____ i _____

Combining Dependent and Independent Clauses

Skillful writers often use subordinating conjunctions to combine related ideas. This strategy also helps writers avoid the choppy effect created by putting too many short sentences in a single paragraph. The subordinating conjunctions include words like *as, if, since, until,* and *whether.*

Combine the sentences using a subordinating conjunction. Write the sentence on the line.

1. Plato was a famous philosopher. Aristotle decided to attend his school.

_____

2. Plato died. Aristotle opened his own school to continue Plato's teachings.

_____

3. An earthquake occurs. Tidal waves begin to form after that.

_____

4. Find shelter. Otherwise, you will be in great danger.

_____

5. The highest number on the Richter scale is a 9. No earthquake has ever been recorded at that level.

_____

_____

6. Architects try to make their designs strong. Earthquakes can be so damaging.

_____

_____

7. The Richter scale is useful. It measures the magnitude of an earthquake.

_____

8. Pasha growled and whined. Cassie knew something was wrong.

_____

9. Pasha paced the living room floor. He barked at Cassie.

_____

Compound Sentences

A **compound sentence** contains two or more simple sentences. The simple sentences are usually joined by a comma and a **coordinating conjunction** such as *and, but, or, for, nor, so,* or *yet.* A second way to join the simple sentences is to place a semicolon between them.

Examples: Friction makes meteors incredibly hot, and they burn up miles above Earth's surface.
Some meteors don't burn completely; they are called meteorites.

Be careful not to confuse a compound sentence with a simple sentence that has a compound subject or compound predicate.

Examples: Rosebud trees and magnolias bloom in the spring. (compound subject)
The three little girls whispered and pointed. (compound predicate)

Read each sentence. Circle *C* if it is a compound sentence. Circle *NC* if it is not a compound sentence.

1. Giraffes and mice have the same number of neck bones—seven.   C   **NC**

2. Kiwi birds have nostrils on their beaks; they can smell earthworms underground.   **C**   NC

3. The pouch under a pelican's bill is huge and can hold up to 25 pounds of fish.   C   **NC**

4. As many as 80,000 honey-producing bees can live together comfortably in one hive.   C   **NC**

5. Most rabbits drown in water, but the marsh rabbit can swim.   **C**   NC

6. Sharks have to keep moving constantly, or they suffocate.   **C**   NC

For each sentence, write *compound subject, compound predicate,* or *compound sentence.*

7. Armadillos are heavy, but they can inflate their stomachs with air to float on water.

_____

8. Llamas, emus, and giraffes have unusually long necks. _____

9. The sloth eats and sleeps while hanging upside down. _____

10. Polar bears feed on seals; seals feed on fish. _____

11. Female penguins usually stay at sea, but they return when their eggs hatch.

_____

12. Elephant mothers pick up their babies with their tusks and carry them from place to place.

_____

Forming Compound Sentences

There are three ways to form compound sentences.

Join the two independent clauses with a coordinating conjunction (*and, but, or, nor, for, so, and yet*). Remember to place a comma before the conjunction.

Example: Most rabbits drown in water, *but* the marsh rabbit can swim.

Insert a semicolon between the two independent clauses.

Example: The grasshopper was green; the cricket was brown.

Connect the two independent clauses with an adverb such as *however, therefore,* or *besides.* Remember to place a semicolon before the adverb and a comma after it.

Example: I'm sure I'll enjoy working with snakes; *besides,* I desperately need the money.

Join these independent clauses using a coordinating conjunction or a semicolon.

1. We can wait for the package. We can leave without it.

   _____

2. I'm driving to the office in an hour. I'll pick up the supplies on the way.

   _____

3. Up went the lottery jackpot. Down went our hopes of winning.

   _____

4. Ava was ready. Her mother was not.

   _____

Connect the two sentences with an adverb from the box below. Write the new sentence on the line.

consequently   still   further   thus   however   therefore   otherwise

5. We should respect our privileges. We might lose them. _____

   _____

6. Scott scrubbed hard for two hours. The walls were not ready to paint. _____

   _____

Complex Sentences

A **complex sentence** consists of one independent clause and at least one dependent clause. A **subordinating conjunction** such as *after, if,* or *when* connects the two clauses into one sentence.

Example: The senators left the capitol after the session was adjourned.

A dependent clause that begins a sentence is usually followed by a comma. If the clause ends the sentence, it usually is not preceded by a comma.

Examples: *Because someone was careless with matches*, a fire started at the Johnsons' home. A fire started at the Johnsons' home *because someone was careless with matches*.

When a dependent clause comes in the middle of a sentence, it is usually set off by commas.

Example: The fire, *which we saw spreading rapidly*, shot sparks into the sky.

Underline the dependent clause in each sentence.

1. When Lena's family made vacation plans, they chose San Francisco as their destination.

2. Because the Harrisons lived in Texas, they traveled by plane.

3. Before the plane landed, the pilot pointed out the Golden Gate Bridge.

4. Mrs. Harrison's parents have lived in San Francisco since they retired.

5. The ride took them to the top of Russian Hill, where they had a great view.

Combine the two sentences into one complex sentence, using proper punctuation to connect the ideas.

6. The Spanish founded San Francisco in 1776. They built a mission and a fort.

   _____

7. The California Gold Rush began in 1848. San Francisco grew rapidly.

   _____

8. The great earthquake and fire of 1906 destroyed much of San Francisco. The city was quickly rebuilt.

   _____

   _____

9. Foggy weather is common in June and July. Most people don't mind it.

   _____

Compound-Complex Sentences

A **compound-complex sentence** contains two or more independent clauses and at least one dependent clause. The dependent clause can come at the beginning, the middle, or the end of the sentence. The two independent clauses can be joined by a comma and a coordinating conjunction (*and, but, nor, for, or, so,* or *yet*) or by a semicolon.

Examples: When we planned our holiday party, we planned a small one, and we invited only a few friends.

My friend Dennis, who is outgoing and creative, suggested some group games; everyone enjoyed them.

We were expecting only eight people, so we were surprised when six extra guests showed up.

Read each compound-complex sentence. For each sentence, underline each independent clause once and each dependent clause twice.

1. You can talk to me whenever you have a problem, or you can talk to your older sister.

2. As we left the restaurant, rain pelted down, so we rushed back inside.

3. The library didn't have the book that Sara needed, so she looked for it online.

4. Since daylight saving time ended, the sky gets dark early, and the days seem a lot shorter.

5. The girls took a walk even though the day was chilly; their mom gave them hot soup when they returned.

Read each sentence. Circle *CD-CX* if it is a compound-complex sentence. Circle *NOT CD-CX* if it is not a compound-complex sentence.

6. When she was young, Keisha roller-skated on sidewalks, and she begged for ice skates.   CD-CX   NOT CD-CX

7. Her parents could not afford skates, which were very expensive, but they encouraged her to earn money herself.   CD-CX   NOT CD-CX

8. Before the week was out, Keisha had found several odd jobs that would pay a few dollars each.   CD-CX   NOT CD-CX

9. She had to apply discipline, but she was able to save almost every dollar.   CD-CX   NOT CD-CX

10. After she bought her own skates, Keisha began skating in competitions, and she even won a few trophies.   CD-CX   NOT CD-CX

Avoiding Run-on Sentences

A **run-on sentence** results when two or more sentences are combined without the proper punctuation to separate them.

Example: It was only three blocks to the restaurant we decided to walk.

A careful writer can correct run-on sentences in several ways:
Make two sentences.
If they are closely related, join the two clauses with a semicolon.
Join the two clauses with a comma and a coordinating conjunction.
Subordinate one clause to the other.
Combine ideas by using appositives and phrases.

Example: The city council held a meeting a meeting is held every month.

The city council holds a meeting every month.

Rewrite each run-on sentence. Use each of the ways listed at least once.

1. The members of our city council are elected by the voters there are two thousand voters in the city.

_____

_____

2. There is one council member from each suburb the president is elected by the council members.

_____

_____

3. The current president of the council is Olivia Saenz she was elected last year.

_____

4. No one believed that Ms. Saenz could win her supporters began to work on her campaign.

_____

5. The council discusses many issues every issue is decided by the full council.

_____

6. Money is needed for many special activities the council plans fund-raisers in the city.

_____

Avoiding Wordiness

Careful writers use as few words as possible to relate their message clearly and precisely. They avoid using extra words or using fancy words where simple ones will do. Good writers also avoid redundancy, or unnecessary repetition.

Underline the unnecessary or repetitive words in each sentence. Rewrite the sentence clearly using as few words as possible.

1. What I want to say is that starfish are fascinating creatures.

   _____

2. A starfish has little feet tipped with suction cups that have suction power.

   _____

3. At the end of each arm is a sensitive eyespot, which is very sensitive.

   _____

4. In spite of the fact that the eyespot cannot really see things, it can tell light from dark.

   _____

5. Starfish come in a variety of colors, shapes, and sizes, and some are bigger than others.

   _____

Underline the wordy language in each sentence.

6. To get to Wilma's house, follow the directions that are written below for you to follow.

7. The first thing you do is get onto Highway 42 and take it to the Sun Drive exit.

8. Turn left and follow Sun Drive, which goes in a northerly direction.

9. Continue driving for four miles, and then turn left at the stop sign.

10. Follow the narrow dirt road for about 1.3 miles approximately.

11. Look for a bright yellow ribbon tied to a tree on the left side of the road as you drive along.

12. Wilma's house is the large white house sitting right there beyond the tree.

13. Rewrite the directions above, making them less wordy. Write the revised directions in a paragraph.

    _____

    _____

Unit 3: Mechanics
Capitalization

Begin every sentence and the first word of a quotation with a capital letter.

Example: The student exclaimed, "How can I ever get my paper done by Friday?"

Capitalize proper nouns and proper adjectives.

Example: Charles Dickens is my favorite author of Victorian literature.

Capitalize the first, last, and all important words in the titles of books, poems, stories, songs, and movies.

Examples: *The Westing Game*   "The Raven"   *Lord of the Rings*

Underline each word that should be capitalized.

1. my brother miguel plays guitar in a band.

2. The name of the band is las muchachas; its theme song is *la bamba*.

3. The lead singer, rosanna, sings some songs in spanish and some in english.

4. Last year, Mary Kate meyers found the band its first job.

5. The band played for a high school dance in cascade, washington, on valentine's day.

6. the dance was sponsored by the cascaders glee club.

7. If I finish my report on ray bradbury, I can go to heron lake next weekend.

8. Anthony said, "what time does *harry potter and the goblet of fire* start?"

9. francis Scott Key wrote "the star-spangled banner."

10. The book *holes* was written by texan louis sachar in 1998.

11. The librarian stated, "that book won the newbery medal in 1999."

12. It was published by Farrar, straus & giroux, which is based in New York.

Write a sentence to show each of these uses of capital letters.

13. name of a restaurant in your community _____

14. a direct quotation _____

15. name of a college or university _____

16. name of a country _____

More About Capitalization

Capitalize a personal title when it precedes a person's name. Also capitalize the abbreviation of the title.

Examples: Governor Shelton   Ms. Piercy   Justice Ginsburg   Dr. Garza

Capitalize the names of days and months, along with their abbreviations.

Examples: Saturday   Sat.   December   Dec.

Capitalize abbreviations used in addresses. Capitalize both letters in the abbreviations of state names.

Examples: St.   Ave.   Blvd.   CA   TX   FL

Rewrite each sentence using correct capitalization.

1. "the bravest people in the world are Doctors," rani said.

   _____

2. She continued, "indira, my stepsister, has been working in calcutta since march."

   _____

3. "Does she work at mercy major hospital or at Calcutta general?" Ben asked.

   _____

4. "Actually, indira is a Specialist in internal medicine at the Clinic on empire street," answered Rani.

   _____

5. "Indira once worked with mother Theresa, the famous albanian nun," Rani finished proudly.

   _____

Underline each word and abbreviation that should be capitalized.

6. silvas high school science fair
   thur., nov. 10th, 9 A.M.
   328 n. canyon blvd.

7. danton water festival
   july 19–21
   brighton dam
   lakeview, mn 67104

8. jeannette duran
   347 antero st.
   markham, ontario L3R 1ES

9. capt. c. j. hatori
   c/o *ocean star*
   p.o. box 5523
   gateway, nh 07621

Plural Nouns

A **plural noun** names more than one person, place, thing, or idea. Most plural nouns are formed by adding *s* or *es* to the singular form. There are, however, many exceptions to this rule.

Examples: word—word*s*   watch—watch*es*   party—par*ties*   shelf—shel*ves*

A few nouns have **irregular plural** forms. Some even keep the same form for both singular and plural.

Examples: child—*children*   trout—*trout*

Write the plural form of the nouns in parentheses on the lines.

1. (wish) In a game my family plays, we each have three _____.

2. (safe) My practical sister always wants three _____ filled with money.

3. (tax) Once, she also asked for one million dollars with no _____.

4. (hero) I always ask to meet all my _____.

5. (peach) Juan, who enjoys desserts, asked for a basket of _____.

6. (kiss) My baby sister asked for 100 hugs and _____.

7. (key) Creativity is one of the _____ to being a good wish-maker.

8. (personality) What people wish for tells a great deal about their _____.

9. (vacation) Mama sometimes wishes for separate _____ for her and her children.

10. (woman) My guess is that many _____ silently wish for the same thing.

Circle the correct plural noun and use it in a sentence.

11. deers   deer   deerses

    _____

12. handfuls   handsful   handsfuls

    _____

13. oxes   oxs   oxen

    _____

Possessive Nouns

A **possessive noun** shows ownership or possession. An **apostrophe (')** is used to form a possessive noun. To form the possessive of most **singular nouns**, add an apostrophe and *s*.

Examples: the symphonies *of Beethoven* = *Beethoven's* symphonies

the lead singer *of the band* = the *band's* lead singer

To form the possessive of a **plural noun** that does not end in *s*, add an apostrophe and *s*. If the plural noun does end in *s*, add only an apostrophe.

Examples: the escape route *of the mice* = the *mice's* escape route

the courage *of the citizens* = the *citizens'* courage

Identify which groups of words in these sentences could be replaced with possessive nouns. Then, rewrite each sentence using the possessive form.

1. The feet of a hummingbird are so weak that the bird never walks. _____

_____

2. The feet of hyraxes form suction cups to climb trees. _____

_____

3. The feet of a sloth are specialized for hanging in trees. _____

_____

4. The forefeet of giraffes are used for kicking predators. _____

_____

5. The body of a centipede can have 95 pairs of legs. _____

_____

6. The paws of pandas have "thumbs" that help them grasp bamboo shoots. _____

_____

Write the plural form of each noun. Then, write the possessive form of the plural noun.

7. goose   _____   _____

8. wolf   _____   _____

9. spy   _____   _____

Commas

As with all punctuation marks, **commas** help writers clarify their meaning and prevent confusion.

Examples: To be successful firefighters must continue to study new methods of first aid. (unclear)

To be successful, firefighters must continue to study new methods of first aid. (clear)

Rules about comma use are numerous. Here are a few.
Use a comma after a word or phrase that introduces a sentence.
Use a comma to set off the name or title of a person who is spoken to directly.
Use commas to set off words or phrases that interrupt the flow of the sentence.
Use commas to set off nonrestrictive appositives.

Correct each sentence by inserting commas where necessary.

1. My favorite instrument the trumpet has a long history.

2. Trumpets in fact are at least 3,500 years old.

3. Silver and bronze trumpets were found in the tomb of Tutankhamen the boy pharaoh of ancient Egypt.

4. In the opinion of many experts these trumpets were used for royal ceremonies.

5. Originally however trumpets could sound only one or two notes.

6. In very ancient times bones and reeds were hollowed out to make trumpets.

7. By 1400 though the straight trumpet was bent into an S-shape.

8. Later I've read it became a single-form loop.

9. According to the encyclopedia valves came into use only in the nineteenth century.

10. I asked Mr. Ortega our band leader about the trumpet.

11. "Mr. Ortega when did you learn to play the trumpet?"

12. "My uncle a fine trumpet player taught me when I was only ten years old."

13. "Who are your favorite trumpeters sir?"

14. "Perry the greatest masters of the trumpet include Louis Armstrong and Miles Davis."

15. "You know Perry some jazz trumpeters also play classical music."

16. "Wynton Marsalis for example is a fine classical musician."

More About Commas

Use a comma to separate words, phrases, or clauses in a series.

Examples: The baby seemed happy, alert, playful, and active.

There were fingerprints on the top, on the sides, and on the bottom.

Use a comma to separate coordinate adjectives used before a noun.

Example: Newfoundlands are large, affectionate dogs.

Do not use a comma between the adjectives if the final adjective is thought of as part of the noun, or if the second adjective carries more weight than the first.

Examples: A huge horned owl lives in those woods.

Jenna received a new silver bracelet as a gift.

Correct each sentence by inserting commas where necessary. If a sentence is already correct, write C on the line.

1. The astronomer explained that a white dwarf is a tiny dense star. _____

2. The captain entered the cockpit checked the instruments and prepared for takeoff. _____

3. The man's sunken weathered face seemed to tell a story of hardship. _____

4. I chose the gift Micah wrapped it and Jeremy gave it to Kelly. _____

5. An unshaded electric light hung from the ceiling. _____

6. Bruce found an old worn-out medicine bag in the barn. _____

7. The neighbors searched behind the garages in the bushes and along the road. _____

8. Their adventure began on a cold drizzly September morning. _____

9. Eleanor Roosevelt's courage humanity and service will always be remembered. _____

10. We drove through the green rolling hills of Pennsylvania. _____

11. Buffalo Bill was a Pony Express rider a scout and a touring stunt performer. _____

12. The hammer the anvil and the stirrup are parts of the human ear. _____

13. The Klines have adopted a beautiful Persian cat from the shelter. _____

14. I like Brandon because he is a warm-hearted considerate person. _____

15. Carla sneaked in and left a huge beautiful fragrant bouquet on the desk. _____

16. Rufus can roll over walk on his hind feet and catch a tennis ball. _____

Commas in Compound and Complex Sentences

A compound sentence contains two or more simple sentences that are connected by a coordinating conjunction such as *and*, *but*, *or*, *for*, *nor*, *yet*, or *so*. Place a comma in front of the conjunction to punctuate the sentence correctly.

Example: Some dinosaurs of the Mesozoic Era were ferocious, *but* others were peaceful.

A complex sentence contains one independent clause and at least one dependent clause. If the dependent clause comes at the beginning or in the middle of the sentence, it is usually set off by commas.

Examples: *Although Plateosaurus was huge,* other reptiles were much more savage.

Other reptiles, *which were smaller than the huge Plateosaurus*, were quite savage.

Do not set off the dependent clause with commas if it is essential to the meaning of the sentence.

Example: The era *that came after the Mesozoic Era* is called the Cenozoic Era.

Correct each sentence by inserting commas where necessary.

1. While human beings must study to become architects some animals build amazing structures by instinct.

2. The male gardener bower bird builds a complex structure and then he decorates it to attract a mate.

3. This bird constructs a dome-shaped garden in a small tree and underneath the tree he lays a carpet of moss.

4. After he covers the moss with brilliant flowers he gathers twigs and arranges them in a circle around the display.

5. Tailor ants which might be called the ant world's high-rise workers gather leaves and sew them around tree twigs to make their nests.

6. These nests which are built in tropical trees may be one hundred feet or more above the ground.

7. Adult tailor ants don't secrete the silk used to weave the leaves together but they squeeze it from their larvae.

8. After the female European water spider builds a waterproof nest under water she stocks the nest with air bubbles.

9. This air supply is very important for it allows the spider to hunt underwater.

10. The water spider lays her eggs in the waterproof nest and they hatch there.

Semicolons

Use a **semicolon (;)** to join independent clauses if they are not joined by *and, but, for, nor, or, so,* or *yet.*

Example: The hurricane lashed the house with gale-force winds; we were scared out of our wits.

Use a semicolon between clauses of a compound sentence that are joined by connecting words such as *therefore, however, thus,* and *then.* Put a comma after the connecting word.

Example: Citizens were warned to evacuate the area; nevertheless, we refused to leave.

Rewrite these sentences, adding semicolons and commas where necessary.

1. Caring for a pet is a big responsibility it takes a lot of time and effort. _____

    _____

2. My dog Homer is my best friend however I get angry with him occasionally. _____

    _____

3. Homer is like all dogs he can be a pest sometimes. _____

    _____

4. A cat fell from a boat into the lake Homer jumped right in after it. _____

    _____

5. Homer can be noisy, dirty, and disobedient still he is irresistible. _____

    _____

Write your own sentences using the connecting word given. Use semicolons and commas correctly.

6. however _____

    _____

7. therefore _____

    _____

8. nevertheless _____

    _____

Colons, Dashes, and Parentheses

Use a **colon (:)** to introduce a series and to separate hours and minutes when expressing time. A colon is also placed after the greeting in a business letter.

Example: The student brought three things to class: the textbook, writing materials, and a willingness to learn.

Use a **dash (—)** to mark a sudden change or break in thought or speech.

Example: The shelter—made of branches, vegetation, and palm strips—was barely adequate for survival.

Use **parentheses ( )** around words or phrases that break into the main thought of a sentence but are not of major importance.

Example: Italian astronomer Galileo (1564–1642) was detained and questioned during the Spanish Inquisition.

Rewrite these sentences, adding colons, parentheses, and dashes where necessary.

1. Animals need care in the following areas shelter, food, exercise, and grooming.

   _____

2. I am responsible for these chores feeding the dog, walking him, and sweeping up the dog hair.

   _____

3. I have to walk our dog, Homer, at 630 every morning.

   _____

4. Sometimes Homer watch out! can be very destructive.

   _____

5. Our previous dog, Cuthbert 1998–2012, was not nearly as accident-prone as Homer is.

   _____

6. Of course, Cuthbert was a different kind of dog about 80 pounds worth of different!

   _____

7. Another curious thing Homer is very fond of our vet.

   _____

Titles of Documents

Capitalize the first word, last word, and all important words in a title.

Put quotation marks around the titles of short works, such as poems, short stories, chapters of books, articles, and songs.

Examples: "The Road Not Taken," "Rock Steady," "The Tell-Tale Heart"

Underline the titles of books, plays, magazines, newspapers, television shows, and movies. If you are using a computer to write, replace underlining with italics.

Examples: People, Chicago Tribune, Sounder   *People, Chicago Tribune, Sounder*

Rewrite the sentences, adding capital letters, quotation marks, and underlines where they are needed.

1. In English class this year, we studied Lois Lowry's novel the giver.

   _____

2. In the library, Gil found a copy of Laurence Yep's book dragon's gate.

   _____

3. Kara liked Langston Hughes's poem long trip.

   _____

4. Maria's favorite short story was after twenty years by O. Henry.

   _____

5. The story machine is a play by Isaac Asimov.

   _____

6. I like the magazine newsweek.

   _____

Read each title, noting the kind of work it is. Rewrite each title correctly.

7. it's a wonderful life (movie) _____

8. a young style for an old story (newspaper article) _____

9. getting to know you (song) _____

10. the song of the moon (poem) _____

Direct Quotations and Dialogue

Use quotation marks before and after the exact words of a speaker.

Example: "The truth is powerful and will prevail," said Sojourner Truth.

If a quote is interrupted by other words, place the quotation marks around the quoted words only. Use a comma to separate the quotation from the rest of the sentence.

Example: "Give me liberty," cried Patrick Henry, "or give me death!"

Place a question mark or an exclamation point inside closing quotation marks only if the quotation itself is a question or an exclamation.

Example: "Haven't you ever heard of Sojourner Truth or Patrick Henry?" asked Marcia.

Rewrite these sentences, inserting correct capitalization, punctuation, and quotation marks.

1. Queen Elizabeth I ruled a great empire, said Marcia.

   _____

2. She told her critics, I have the heart and stomach of a king.

   _____

3. Who else had a great impact on a country? asked Terri.

   _____

4. Well, Ben remarked, Mohandas Gandhi inspired a nonviolent revolution in India.

   _____

   _____

5. Write the dialogue correctly. Remember to start a new paragraph each time the speaker changes.

   Teach me how to play chess said Devon. What are these eight small pieces called he questioned. Those pieces, Sarah answered, are called pawns. They are the weakest pieces on the chessboard. How about the queen asked Devon. Now the queen is a different story. She can move in any direction until her path is blocked Sarah explained. So Devon reasoned if your queen is captured, I guess you're in real trouble. Not necessarily Sarah replied. I've won games with only two bishops and a rook.

   _____

   _____

   _____

Continue on your own paper.

Abbreviations, Acronyms, and Initialisms

An **abbreviation** is a short way of writing something. Common abbreviations include those for units of measure (*doz, Hz, in., lb*), personal titles (*Dr., Capt., Ms.*), dates and times (*A.M., Oct., Mon.*), and postal terms (*TX, St., CA, Ave.*).

An **acronym** is a kind of abbreviation. Acronyms are formed from the first letters of a series of words, and they always create a pronounceable word. **Initialisms** are similar to acronyms because they are also formed from the first letters of a series of words. Initialisms are *not*, however, pronounced as a word.

Acronyms: *RAM* (random access memory)
                 NASA (National Aeronautics and Space Administration)

Initialisms: PTA (Parent Teacher Association)   USA (United States of America)

Write the abbreviation of each term. Use a dictionary if necessary.

1. Fahrenheit _____

2. New Mexico _____

3. 2.5 milliliters _____

4. Governor Smith _____

5. National Basketball Association _____

6. miles per hour _____

7. Central Intelligence Agency _____

8. Incorporated _____

The underlined abbreviations would be more appropriately written out since each is a part of a sentence. On the lines, write the word or words that were abbreviated.

9. I read an article about sharks in the <u>Sept.</u> issue of a science magazine. _____

10. The largest shark in the ocean, the white shark, measures up to 49 <u>ft</u> in length. _____

11. The smallest shark measures only 15–20 <u>cm</u> in length. _____

12. Some of my friends have seen sharks off the coast of <u>FL.</u> _____

Write out the words that the abbreviations stand for. Then, write *acronym* or *initialism* to identify the kind of abbreviation.

13. FBI _____

14. scuba _____

15. U.N. _____

16. ROM _____

Contractions

Form **contractions** by joining two words together and replacing one or more letters with an apostrophe.

Examples: is not = isn't   they will = they'll   who is (or who has) = who's

Be careful when you write sentences that contain contractions formed with the word *not* (*can't, won't, didn't*). These contractions are negatives, so you must avoid putting another negative word in the same sentence.

Examples: *Nobody can't* tell the twins apart. (double negative—incorrect)

   Nobody can tell the twins apart. (correct)

Rewrite each sentence, using the correct contraction.

1. Are you not the novelist who wrote this book?

   _____

2. In my opinion, the photo on your book's jacket will not be any advantage to you.

   _____

3. Why can new novelists not have some common sense?

   _____

4. Perhaps you can take advice from someone who has got experience.

   _____

5. You will be sorry for putting a grinning photo on your book.

   _____

6. I have got only one author photo on my shelf—this one of myself.

   _____

Write the contraction for each pair of words.

7. did not _____   10. who is _____

8. will not _____   11. does not _____

9. she is _____   12. she has _____

Unit 4: Vocabulary and Usage
Word Parts

Many words are made up of smaller units called **word parts**. The **root** is the part of the word that carries the word's core meaning. Sometimes it is called the **base word.**

*Examples: graph*ic *mot*ion *sym*pathy sus*pend*

A **prefix** is a word part that is added to the beginning of a word to change the meaning.

*Examples: dis*appear *in*definite *mis*manage *re*arrange

A **suffix** is a word part that is added to the end of a word to change the meaning.

Examples: worth*less* kind*ness* break*able* educa*tion*

Some words have both a prefix and a suffix.

*Examples: un*forgett*able im*possibili*ty dis*respect*ful* re*creation

Examine the parts of each underlined word to figure out its meaning. Fill in the blanks correctly, and write a definition of the word.

1. The armadillo is a prehistoric creature with distinctive armor but an underdeveloped brain.

   The prefix _____ means "before," and the suffix _____ means

   "relating to." The definition of *prehistoric* is _____.

2. After hiding my slippers and shredding the newspaper, my unrepentant puppy wagged his tail and fell asleep.

   The prefix _____ means "not," and the suffix _____ means

   "inclined to." The definition of *unrepentant* is _____.

3. Many environmental groups are concerned about the deforestation of Central America.

   The prefix _____ means "down" or "away," and the suffix

   _____ means "the act of." The definition of *deforestation* is

   _____.

4. The coexistence of cowbirds and livestock illustrates how mammals adapt to one another in nature.

   The prefix _____ means "together," and the suffix _____

   means "the act of." The definition of *coexistence* is _____.

58

Latin and Greek Prefixes, Suffixes, and Roots

Many roots, prefixes, and suffixes come from ancient Latin and Greek words.

Examples:

Word Part	Origin	Meaning
-prim- (root)	Latin	first, early
-graph- (root)	Greek	write, writing, study
inter- (prefix)	Latin	between, among
hemi- (prefix)	Greek	half
-tude (suffix)	Latin and Greek	quality, state

Knowing the meanings of some common Greek and Latin word parts can help you figure out the meanings of unfamiliar words.

Use the chart to figure out the meaning of each word below, and write the definition on the line. Check your definitions in a dictionary.

Roots	Meaning	Suffixes	Meaning
-aud-	hear	-ate	to become, to cause to be
-bio-	life	-fy	make, cause
-dict-	say	-ible	able, likely
-log-	study, word	-tion	action, condition
magn-	large		

1. biology _____

2. magnify _____

3. diction _____

4. audible _____

5. dictate _____

Use the hint in parentheses to guess the meaning of the underlined word. Check your definitions in a dictionary.

6. That basket has a detachable handle. (The prefix *de-* means "off." The suffix *–able* means "able.")

_____

7. Working in a hospital, Hector used antibacterial soap many times each day. (The prefix *anti-* means

"against.")_____

Compounds, Blends, and Clipped Words

A **compound word** is made up of two smaller words. **Open compounds** are written as separate words; **closed compounds** are written as one word. **Hyphenated compounds** have hyphens between the smaller words.

Examples: post office   newspaper   baby-sitter

A **blend** is a combination of parts of words into one word.

Examples: swipe (sweep + wipe)   slang (slovenly + language)   Medicare (medicine + care)

A **clipped word** is a shortened version of a longer word.

Examples: limo (limousine)   max (maximum)   demo (demonstration)

Underline the compounds, blends, and clipped words in the paragraph. Label the compound words CP, the blends BL, and the clipped words CL.

Homecoming weekend for the alums of Madison Prep was an outstanding success. Previous

classmates, now meeting as grown-ups, held their reunion in the ivied hallways that their forebears had used

for generations. Since most alums arrived at the dorms late and slept in, the first event of the day was

brunch. The chair of the event had asked the servers to dress in the uniforms the alums had worn when they

attended prep school. The women, some with their hair in ponytails, gossiped about old boyfriends.

Meanwhile, the old baseball team took on the basketball team in a fierce Hearts tournament. In the late

afternoon, when farewells were said, more than a few tears glittered on smiling faces.

Write the correct blend on the lines.

1. motor + hotel = _____

2. splash + spatter = _____

3. flame + glare = _____

4. international + network = _____

5. marionette + puppet = _____

6. prim + sissy = _____

7. smoke + fog = _____

8. fourteen + nights = _____

9. sky + laboratory = _____

10. parachute + troops = _____

11. dance + exercise = _____

12. network + etiquette = _____

Synonyms

> **Synonyms** are words that have similar meanings.
> *Examples:*   tale, story, myth, legend, fantasy, parable, yarn

Write one synonym for the underlined word in each sentence.

1. As a child, did you ever play with a <u>strange</u> molding material? _____

2. Who came up with the idea to <u>make</u> some gooey stuff for children to mold? _____

3. The answer is that <u>nobody</u> did! _____

4. In the early 1940s, U.S. companies were searching for a <u>cheap</u> substitute for rubber. _____

5. An engineer named James Wright succeeded in creating <u>fake</u> rubber. _____

6. It could <u>stretch</u> more than rubber did. _____

7. Molds and decay did not <u>harm</u> it, and it bounced 25 percent higher than a real rubber ball.

   _____

8. Unfortunately, this new "stuff," while <u>interesting</u>, had no real practical advantages over rubber.

   _____

9. <u>Employees</u> at the lab called the new stuff "nutty putty" and showed it to people who came to visit.

   _____

Read the paragraph. Write a synonym for each underlined word in the space provided.

Marcus was (10) <u>afraid</u> of tarantulas. He didn't care that people (11) <u>said</u> tarantulas were actually harmless. He was (12) <u>repulsed</u> by the thought of their huge, hairy bodies. Marcus had heard that in Texas they crawled along <u>walls</u> and (13) <u>hung</u> from ceilings. Having this (14) <u>information</u> was enough to make Marcus's skin crawl.

10. _____

11. _____

12. _____

13. _____

14. _____

Name _____ Date _____

Antonyms

Antonyms are words that have opposite meanings.
Examples: adult—child   start—stop   fresh—stale   quickly—slowly

Write two antonyms for each word.

1. arrive _____ _____

2. tired _____ _____

3. fantastic _____ _____

4. dishonesty _____ _____

5. quickly _____ _____

6. friend _____ _____

7. boring _____ _____

8. conceal _____ _____

9. turbulent _____ _____

10. difficult _____ _____

11. fortunate _____ _____

12. advance _____ _____

Write one synonym and one antonym for each word.

Word	Synonym	Antonym
13. demonstrate		
14. appreciate		
15. leader		
16. confident		
17. establish		
18. frequently		
19. afraid		
20. buy		

Homographs—Words with Multiple Meanings

> **Homographs** are words that are spelled the same but have different meanings. They are often pronounced differently.
>
> *Example:*   The *invalid* has been in the hospital for three months.
>
>   The test has become *invalid* because the standards are different this year.

Underline the homograph in each sentence. Write both meanings of the word on the line.

1. From studying the minute patterns in a leaf to hiking along beautiful trails, I enjoyed every minute of

   the camping trip. _____

2. After reviewing the content of my rough draft, my tutor was content with the quality of my paper.

   _____

3. Soldiers who are based in the desert rarely desert their posts because they have no place to go.

   _____

4. The high lead content in some old paint can lead to serious health problems for those exposed to it.

   _____

5. The EMS worker wound a clean, cotton bandage around the victim's chest wound.

   _____

6. The protesters refuse to leave until the council hears their resolution about the correct disposal of

   refuse. _____

7. When the rainstorm began, I dove for cover, and the little dove disappeared into the underbrush.

   _____

8. Advocates of the homeless object to their clients being treated as objects of scorn.

   _____

Write the homograph for each pair of meanings below.

_____ **9.** a. to delay   b. a place for horses

_____ **10.** a. to ease grief   b. a cabinet

_____ **11.** a. to turn   b. air in motion

Homophones

> **Homophones** are words that sound alike but have different meanings and different spellings.
> *Example:*   The recordings of that new rap *band* were *banned* in the United States.

Underline the homophone pair in each sentence.

1. Dad said, "Pack up the tents! I've been feeling tense lately, so we're going camping."

2. I didn't know where we were going, but I knew I had nothing to wear on a camping expedition.

3. Not knowing when the stores would close, I hurried to the mall to look for appropriate clothes.

4. Those days of hiking and swimming and camping went by in a beautiful daze.

Underline the correct homophones in the sentences.

5. The night (air, heir) is (sew, so) cool that you will (knead, need) a light jacket.

6. The small plants were set out in orderly (rows, rose).

7. Lee (seams, seems) to have forgotten about (our, hour) plans for the picnic.

8. I (knew, new) those (knew, new) shoes would hurt my (feat, feet).

9. We did (not, knot) go to the (seen, scene) of the wreck.

10. If this diet succeeds, I (mite, might) be able to fasten this belt around my (waist, waste).

Write the homophone for each word listed below.

11. peace _____

12. principle _____

13. boarder _____

14. billed _____

15. pause _____

16. sum _____

17. bawl _____

18. him _____

19. altar _____

20. meet _____

21. sight _____

22. cent _____

23. way _____

24. guessed _____

25. ate _____

26. blew _____

Context Clues

The **context** of a word consists of the words that surround it. Sometimes the context of an unfamiliar word will give you clues to its meaning. Four common types of **context clues** are **definitions**, **examples**, **synonyms**, and **antonyms**.

Examples: At the center of the ring was a small emerald, which is *a deep-green precious stone.* (definition)

Gems, such as *diamonds*, *sapphires*, and *opals*, are used to make jewelry. (examples)

His *guilt* and *regret* showed that his remorse was real. (synonyms)

Her placid expression showed no sign of how *panic-stricken* she really was. (antonym)

Find the definition for the underlined word in the box, and write the letter on the line. Check your answers in a dictionary.

a. opponents or enemies
b. fragments of destroyed objects
c. very clean and neat
d. sea animals with hard outer shells

_____ **1.** Digging through the ruins left by the storm, they found the dog under some debris and rescued him.

_____ **2.** Unlike her sister Flora, who is sloppy, Elena is always fastidious.

_____ **3.** Crustaceans such as shrimp, lobsters, and crayfish are popular food items.

_____ **4.** They had been political adversaries, or foes, throughout their careers.

Use context clues to guess the meaning of the underlined word. Write the definition on the line and then check it in a dictionary.

5. The customer wanted to negotiate, or come to verbal agreement, on the price.

_____

6. If you want us to understand every word you say, you will have to speak slowly and enunciate.

_____

7. Ticks, fleas, and other parasites can make your pet miserable.

_____

Denotation and Connotation

The **denotation** of a word is its exact meaning as stated in a dictionary.

The **connotation** of a word is the feeling that a word suggests when it is used. Some words are neutral in connotation; others carry a suggestion that something is positive or negative.

Examples: house (neutral)   home (positive)   hovel (negative)

Use the pairs of words to complete the sentences. Then, write *positive*, *negative*, or *neutral* to indicate the connotation of the word.

left   **abandoned**

1. Before going on vacation, the owners _____ the puppy at the kennel.

   _____

2. Before going on vacation, the owners _____ the puppy at the kennel.

   _____

gaudy   **ornate**

3. The _____ carvings that decorated the mantel made a dramatic impression.

   _____

4. The _____ carvings that decorated the mantel made a dramatic impression.

   _____

paintings   **masterpieces**

5. The *Mona Lisa* is one of Leonardo da Vinci's _____.

   _____

6. The *Mona Lisa* is one of Leonardo da Vinci's _____.

   _____

loud   **enthusiastic**

7. A group of _____ regulars eats at Arno's every Friday night.

   _____

8. A group of _____ regulars eats at Arno's every Friday night.

   _____

Idioms

An **idiom** is a group of words that has a different meaning from the literal definition of its parts. Idioms are often colorful expressions used in speech and in informal writing, but they should be used carefully in formal writing.

Examples: People can *get into hot water* when they speak before they think. (idiom)

People can *make serious mistakes* when they speak before they think.
(more formal sentence)

Underline the idiom in each sentence. Rewrite the sentence, substituting other words in place of the underlined idioms. Make any changes necessary.

1. For our English assignment, we are to list all the idioms we come across as we read.

   _____

2. Because I have spoken English for only three years, understanding idioms is hardly a piece of cake

   for me. _____

   _____

3. Nevertheless, I have come a long way in the past three years.

   _____

4. Marta thinks works of modern fiction are the best bet for finding idioms.

   _____

5. Because I need to make a good grade, I'm going to take my time finishing the assignment.

   _____

6. Marta says I will get the hang of it if I concentrate on the exact meaning of each word.

   _____

7. Fortunately, my tutor is willing to bend over backwards to help me improve my English.

   _____

8. In the long run, studying idioms will help me to better understand my new language.

   _____

Clichés

> A **cliché** is a word or phrase that has become overused and, therefore, no longer communicates effectively. Clichés come to mind easily because they are familiar. However, they are usually wordy and vague. Clichés should be used sparingly in formal writing.
>
> *Example:*   Run it up the flagpole. (cliché)
>
>   See what others think. (better expression of the idea)

Underline the cliché in each sentence. Rewrite the sentences as much as is necessary to express the ideas more effectively.

1. In business, profit is usually the bottom line.

   _____

2. The estimated cost of adding to the product line is a ballpark figure.

   _____

3. Since this is the final year of the project, let's go out in a blaze of glory.

   _____

4. That strange new scooter design will never see the light of day.

   _____

5. The customer rejected the sketches, so the architects are back to square one.

   _____

6. These are the winning lottery numbers, beyond a shadow of a doubt.

   _____

7. Production will grind to a halt if the rumored layoffs occur.

   _____

8. The university's new computer system provides state-of-the-art technology.

   _____

9. Using nonstandard English is a definite no-no.

   _____

Name _____ Date _____

Figurative Language

Figurative language, such as similes and metaphors, can add information and clarify meaning in new and creative ways. A **simile** compares two unlike things using the word *like* or *as*. A **metaphor** compares two unlike things without using *like* or *as*.

Examples: Above, the stars were *as bright as headlights.* (simile)

Above, the stars were *headlights, guiding our steps.* (metaphor)

Complete each sentence using figurative language. Circle *S* if the sentence is a simile or *M* if it is a metaphor.

1. S M   The old book was as dusty as _____

_____

2. S M   The poem about the homeless was a _____

_____

3. S M   The people snorted and stomped in the snow like _____

_____

4. S M   A boat slipped by in the fog like _____

_____

5. S M   On the dark highway, the toll booth was a _____

_____

6. S M   In my imagination, the foreign land was a _____

_____

7. S M   With her nose buried in a book, she looked like _____

_____

8. S M   When he unwrapped the new book, his face lit up like _____

_____

9. S M   The chariot was a _____

_____

10. S M   The horn of the freighter cut through the night like _____

_____

More Figurative Language

Figurative language helps a writer express meaning in fresh or creative ways.

An **allusion** is a reference to a person, place, or event from history, literature, religion, mythology, sports, science, or popular culture.

Example: My brother loves science and is getting a reputation as a real Einstein.

A **hyperbole** uses obvious exaggeration to emphasize a point, express strong emotion, or create a comic effect. Hyperboles are not meant to be taken literally.

Example: I am so tired I could sleep for a million years.

Write allusion or hyperbole to identify the type of figurative language.

1. By the end of the day we had a pile of leaves a mile high. _____

2. Jamal has enough friends to fill a basketball arena. _____

3. Kevin tried to get Corrine's attention by being a Romeo. _____

4. I will need some help to complete this challenging project; I can't part the Red Sea all

   by myself. _____

5. The hole in the ground was so deep we could see China if we squinted. _____

6. The geese we saw at the lake were as big as houses. _____

7. My little brother, or Yoda as I like to call him, is incredibly wise for such a small child.

   _____

8. Ethan's new boss turned out to be the Big Bad Wolf disguised as Grandma. _____

9. My aunt always tells us, "You don't have to be Picasso to enjoy creating art." _____

10. It's so cold even the penguins need sweaters. _____

Complete each sentence using a hyperbole.

11. Those "giant" pizzas at Mario's are the size of _____.

12. The early morning sun was so bright that _____.

13. They were tired after waiting at the train station _____.

14. Wow! That trail of ants must have been _____ long!

15. I still love this jacket even though it's older than _____.

Subject–Verb Agreement

A subject and verb must agree in number. Use the singular form of a verb with a singular subject and the plural form with a plural subject. Remember that most collective and mass nouns take a singular verb.

Example: A large *crowd is expected.* The *grass is growing* rapidly.

Sometimes a prepositional phrase lies between the subject and verb. Remember that the verb must agree with the sentence's subject, not with the object of the preposition.

Example: The *colors* in the painting *are* vivid.

A compound subject joined by *and* requires a plural verb. When a compound subject is joined by *or* or *nor*, the verb must agree with the subject closest to the verb.

Example: The student or her *parents are required* to sign the release form.

Write the correct verb on the line.

1. (is, are) Hard work and a good attitude _____ important to us.

2. (is, are) The good news _____ our winning record.

3. (give, gives) Headlines usually _____ credit to a particular goal or save.

4. (is, are) Teamwork _____ really the winner.

5. (deserve, deserves) The pep squad _____ some of the credit, too.

6. (understand, understands) Each of us _____ team spirit.

7. (work, works) We all _____ together.

Write a predicate to complete each sentence. Use a verb in the present tense.

8. The coaches at our school _____.

9. My soccer coach _____.

10. The soccer team _____.

11. The crowd _____.

12. Neither the players nor the coach _____.

13. The team uniforms _____.

14. The season _____.

15. Most of the equipment _____.

Avoiding Double Negatives

Nonstandard English is always wrong for the writing you do in school unless you are creating dialogue. Using double negatives is nonstandard English and must be avoided.

A **negative** is a word that means "no" or "not." Contractions that end in *n't* are negatives.

Examples: never, no one, neither, barely, hardly, don't, won't, can't

A **double negative** occurs when a writer puts two or more negative words in the same sentence.

Example: *No one* should *never* drive on ice. (double negative)

No one should ever drive on ice. (correct English)

Underline the negatives in each sentence. Rewrite sentences that contain a double negative. Write *correct* if the sentence does not contain a double negative.

1. Hardly nobody knows about the mummy the Russians found in Siberia.

   _____

2. Gold prospectors hadn't barely begun digging when they found something strange.

   _____

3. No one had never seen nothing like it.

   _____

4. Nothing like this creature existed except in ancient cave drawings.

   _____

5. Scientists couldn't scarcely believe it—it was a baby mammoth!

   _____

6. Mammoths hadn't existed on Earth for at least 9,000 years.

   _____

7. Although this mammoth was very young when it died, it wasn't no tiny creature.

   _____

8. The prospectors couldn't hardly get the mummy out of the ground.

   _____

Avoiding Nonstandard Verb Forms

Nonstandard English is always wrong for the writing you do in school unless you are creating dialogue. Certain forms of verbs are mistakenly used as correct but are actually nonstandard forms of the verb.

Examples: ain't, growed, throwed

Never use nonstandard verbs. They are incorrect.

Underline the nonstandard verbs. Rewrite the sentences correctly.

1. Our people need good health care, and we ain't about to take no for an answer.

_____

2. The test wasn't as difficult as I expected, but nobody knowed the answer to the bonus question.

_____

3. "Why, look at those kids. They're all growed up!" said Great Aunt Matilda.

_____

4. At the last World Series, the President throwed out the first ball.

_____

5. Frank fell out of the tree and busted his arm.

_____

6. The blind date should have been successful, but the guy brung along his dog!

_____

7. Raymond couldn't believe a 6-year-old drawed the winning raffle ticket.

_____

8. He heared the little girl's feet couldn't even touch the pedals.

_____

9. Hurricanes nearly drownded half of Louisiana this season.

_____

10. The gale-force winds blowed at nearly 70 miles per hour.

_____

Pronoun–Antecedent Agreement

An **antecedent** is the noun or nouns to which a pronoun refers. A pronoun should agree with its antecedent in number and gender.

Examples: In 1847, *Homan Walsh* offered *his* help to some railway engineers. The *engineers* were building a suspension bridge at Niagara Falls, and *they* were having trouble.

Antecedents are often in the same sentence with their pronouns. Sometimes, however, the antecedent is in another sentence.

Example: Heavy *cables* crossed a steep gorge. How to get *them* across the gorge was the problem.

Underline each pronoun, and write its antecedent on the line.

1. As president of the Senate in the 1830s, Martin Van Buren kept a gun near him to maintain order.

   _____

2. During the Civil War, Emma Edmonds spied for the Union after disguising herself as a male slave.

   _____

3. Dr. Mary Walker, a surgeon, tended Union soldiers and spent time with them in a Confederate prison.

   _____

4. "The Battle Hymn of the Republic" was a popular song with Union soldiers as they fought in the Civil War.

   _____

5. The song by Julia Ward Howe was published in a magazine, but she was not named as the author.

   _____

6. Howe, along with her husband Samuel, was the editor of the *Boston Commonwealth*.

   _____

7. Many famous poets of the day voiced their praise for the inspiring lyrics of the song.

   _____

8. Howe's words have remained popular with soldiers, who sang the same song during World War I.

   _____

Write the pronoun that is needed to complete each sentence.

9. Anna Taylor went to Niagara Falls, but _____ crossed them in a very unusual way.

10. Witnesses watched with _____ mouths open.

11. Anna Taylor had squeezed _____ into a barrel.

12. Was Taylor the first person to survive a trip over Niagara Falls? Of course _____ was!

Active Voice and Passive Voice

When a sentence is written in **active voice**, the subject of the sentence performs the action described in the sentence. **Passive voice** means that the subject of the sentence receives the action described in the sentence.

Examples: The *members* of the drill team washed the cars. (active voice)

The subject (*members*) is **performing** the washing.

The *cars* were washed by the members of the drill team. (passive voice)

The subject (*cars*) is **receiving** the action.

Identify each underlined verb as active or passive. Write *A* if the verb is in active voice, *P* if it is in passive voice. Then rewrite each sentence, changing those in active voice to passive voice and vice versa.

_____ 1. Cats inspire writers. _____

_____

_____ 2. Mark Twain's favorite cats were named Beelzebub, Blatherskit, Apollinaris, and Buffalo Bill.

_____

_____

_____ 3. The Cheshire Cat gave Alice orders when she was in Wonderland.

_____

_____ 4. A cat helped Dick Whittington become mayor of London.

_____

_____ 5. The poem "A Naming of Cats" was written by T. S. Eliot.

_____

_____ 6. According to Rudyard Kipling, the cat was first domesticated by a cave woman.

_____

_____ 7. Books about cats are enjoyed by most children.

_____

_____ 8. Dr. Seuss wrote *The Cat in the Hat*, a book which has delighted young children since 1957.

_____

_____

Avoiding Misplaced Modifiers

Modifiers can be words, phrases, or clauses. In sentences, modifiers should be placed near the words they modify so that their meaning is clear. A **misplaced modifier** distorts or muddles sentence meaning.

Examples: The lottery winner *almost* spent $4,000 on a new bicycle.

The lottery winner spent *almost* $4,000 on a new bicycle.

The dog belongs to that man *with the black spots*.

The dog *with the black spots* belongs to that man.

Underline the misplaced modifier in each sentence. Rewrite the sentence to correct the modifier's placement.

1. We talked about the track meet in the cafeteria.

   _____

2. The lynx grows hairs for walking on snow on the bottoms of its feet.

   _____

3. Made from matzo meal, Rachel shapes tasty dumplings.

   _____

4. My friend Tracy visited me who lives in Denver, Colorado.

   _____

5. Swinging wildly from branch to branch, I watched the chimpanzee.

   _____

6. Hoy taught us with chopsticks how to eat rice.

   _____

7. Filled with daisies, the girls walked through the field.

   _____

8. Annie goes jogging in the park when she gets home frequently.

   _____

Avoiding Dangling Modifiers

A **dangling modifier** is a modifier that does not clearly and sensibly modify another word in a sentence.

Examples: *Walking to the bus,* the morning was pleasant. (dangling)

Walking to the bus, I enjoyed the pleasant morning. (modifies *I*)

All bundled up in a blanket, the baby's first outing was a brief one. (dangling)

All bundled up in a blanket, the baby had a brief first outing. (modifies *baby*)

Rewrite each sentence to fix the dangling modifier.

1. When performing on stage, the microphone should not be placed too near the speaker cones.

_____

2. Standing near the runway, the noise of the jets was deafening.

_____

3. Worried, deep creases appeared on Nick's forehead.

_____

4. The missing baseball card was found cleaning my closet.

_____

5. Tired from the long walk through the snow, food and rest were welcomed.

_____

6. Frightened, the rabbit's ears perked up and its nose twitched.

_____

7. To stay healthy and energetic, good nutrition is needed.

_____

8. Mexico City was their home before moving to Pittsburgh.

_____

9. Exploring the cave, a new tunnel was discovered.

_____

Consistent Verb Tenses

> Careful writers avoid shifts in verb tense unless there is good reason.

Rewrite the paragraphs, correcting any sentences containing a verb that is inconsistent with the rest of the paragraph. If there is a good reason for a shift in verb tense, explain it in writing.

1. It was a bitter cold night for speed skating, but the three teams give their all for the regional competition. Most surprising was the performance of Coolidge High, which outskated the other two teams in every category. They are the easy winners.

   _____

   _____

   _____

2. Johnson raced down the court. He stops dead, raises those incredibly long arms, and sinks the ball slow-motion into the basket. He scored 33 points before the final quarter ended.

   _____

   _____

   _____

3. Golf has always been my dad's favorite game. He says it is easygoing, just like he is. He used to spend every Saturday and Sunday on the links when he was my age. He worked as a caddy to earn enough money to play golf himself.

   _____

   _____

   _____

4. I had never seen a rodeo before. I expect the events to be tough and exciting. What I don't expect was the gracefulness and incredible agility involved. I was glued to my seat.

   _____

   _____

   _____

Troublesome Verbs

The verbs in certain verb pairs are frequently confused for each other.

Sit means "to take a seat, as in a chair." *Set* means "to put in a certain place or position."

Rise means "to get up" or "to move higher." *Raise* means "to lift" or "to elevate."

Lie means "to be or remain" or "to recline." *Lay* means "to put or place in a particular position."

Present Tense	Past Tense	Past Participle
lie	lay	(has, have, had) lain
lay	laid	(has, have, had) laid
sit	sat	(has, have, had) sat
set	set	(has, have, had) set
rise	rose	(has, have, had) risen
raise	raised	(has, have, had) raised

Write the verb that completes each sentence correctly.

1. (set, sat) Admiral Zorg _____ at the controls of the starship *Explorer*.

2. (set, sat) He had _____ the velocity of the ship at warp speed 7.

3. (lay, laid) Planet 32 of the Trifton solar system _____ in ruins.

4. (sat, set) The ship's navigator, Lieutenant Maxar, _____ at the admiral's side.

5. (rose, raised) Zorg _____ his arm wearily.

6. (lay, lain) Pointing to the remains of Planet 32, he said, "The volcano had _____ dormant for millennia."

7. (rise, raise) He added, "Who could have predicted that the lava would _____ so suddenly?"

8. (laid, lay) Maxar _____ a complex chart of numbers and symbols on the desk.

9. (lies, lays) "The answer _____ in these calculations, Admiral," he said.

10. (Set, Sit) The admiral nodded sadly. "_____ our course for home," he ordered.

Write a sentence using each of the following verbs correctly.

11. sitting _____

12. setting _____

13. lying _____

14. laying _____

Unit 5: Writing
Writing for an Audience and Purpose

Careful writers are guided by their **purpose** for writing and their intended **audience**.

Each item below names an audience. Circle the letter of the passage that is better adapted for that audience.

1. six-year-olds

    a. The grieving process for the death of a family pet can be almost as stressful as it is for the death of a close relative.

    b. Dogs and cats do not live as long as people do. Sometimes pets die, and that makes us feel terrible.

2. scientists

    a. My cat Binky does the strangest thing! He makes a funny chattering sound whenever he sees a bird.

    b. Wild cats are quiet and stealthy when stalking birds. Pet cats, however, make a chattering sound in their throats.

3. potential adopters of pets

    a. This lovable little bundle of fur will be just like another member of your family.

    b. Canines do require more care than felines. For example, they must be exercised frequently.

Write one paragraph about the responsibilities of caring for a dog or cat for the audience listed.

4. adults: _____

    _____

    _____

    _____

5. fourth graders: _____

    _____

    _____

    _____

Personal Narrative

In a **personal narrative**, the writer tells about an event that the writer participated in or observed. A personal narrative is autobiographical, but it typically focuses on a specific experience. A personal narrative
- is written in the first-person point of view.
- usually reveals or suggests the writer's feelings.
- has a beginning, a middle, and an end.

Read the personal narrative below. Then, answer the questions that follow.

My early art was so bad that my first-grade teacher suggested my vision be tested. When the ophthalmologist gave me a clean bill of health, my parents sent me to an optometrist for eye-hand coordination exercises. Still, none of my artwork was ever posted on the classroom bulletin board.

At home, however, things were different. My parents proudly displayed on the refrigerator nearly every piece of art I ever produced. One time my father had an abstract that especially pleased him framed. Encouraged by my family, I continued to draw. My parents tell me I never seemed to notice that my drawings were very different from those of my classmates.

For my birthday, Granny bought me two books: *How to Draw Animals* and *How to Draw Space Creatures*. I began to practice, used some of the authors' ideas and some of my own, and developed a distinctive style. I started creating the things I'd always seen in my imagination.

1. From what point of view is this narrative told? _____

2. How do you know? _____

_____

3. List the events of the narrative in the order in which they happened.

   a. _____

   b. _____

   c. _____

   d. _____

   e. _____

   f. _____

4. What do you think eventually happens in the writer's life? _____

_____

5. What is the main theme the writer is trying to convey? _____

_____

Name _____ Date _____

Using Dialogue

Skilled writers use dialogue effectively in their personal narratives. Including the real words of real people makes a narrative come alive.

Write a short conversation based on the event described. Remember that different people have different ways of speaking. Make your dialogue sound as natural and as real as possible.

1. A mother and her ten-year-old daughter go on a camping trip. They have found a nice campsite near a lake. The daughter wants to go down to the lake right away, but the mother needs her help setting up the tent and other equipment. To encourage her daughter to help, the mother explains why it is important to set the site up properly. She talks about the activities they can do once they have the site finished. She also finds ways to make the work fun.

_____

_____

_____

_____

_____

2. Two friends, Kyle and Darren, go to the neighborhood park to fly Darren's new kite. As they are getting the kite ready, they notice a younger boy trying to fly a kite by himself. The younger boy gets his kite stuck in a tree, far beyond anyone's reach. Kyle and Darren watch as the little boy sits on the grass, buries his head in his hands, and begins crying. They go over to talk to the boy to try to comfort him.

_____

_____

_____

_____

_____

Using Transitions

Transitions are words or phrases that connect ideas. Careful writers use transitions in their personal narrative to show the sequence of events. Transitions can also be used to show a shift from one time frame or setting to another.

Rewrite the passage from a personal narrative. Use transitions to show the order of events and shifts in setting or time frame. You can use transitions to combine sentences and make the writing smoother.

I will never forget the day I met my best friend Gina. I was only eight years old. It had snowed about a foot. Some kids in the neighborhood were going to go sledding on the hill at the park. My mom bundled me up in a bright red snowsuit. She added a scarf, boots, gloves, and a hat. I felt like I could hardly move! I met some of the sledders near my house, and we headed to the park.

We approached Maple Avenue. A huge St. Bernard came running around the corner. All the other kids ran away, but I tripped on the curb and fell. I could not get up. The dog came and sniffed me and lumbered off. I was lying there, just about to start crying. I heard a kind voice say, "Need a hand?" I looked up and saw a red-headed girl about my age with the broadest smile I had ever seen. She helped me up, introduced herself, and talked so much I forgot about my ordeal.

Her mother made us hot chocolate. We drank it at the kitchen table. Gina told me her life story. I just sat there listening and feeling grateful for my new friend.

_____

_____

_____

_____

_____

_____

_____

_____

_____

_____

_____

_____

_____

Personal Narrative: Graphic Organizer

Plan to write a personal narrative about something you do well. Use the graphic organizer to plan your personal narrative.

What are you going to write about?

⬇

Tell what your skill is, how you learned it, and when you use it.

⬇

Tell how your skill makes your life more interesting.

Personal Narrative: Writing

Tips for Writing a Personal Narrative
- Write from your point of view. Use the words *I, me, my,* and *mine* to show your readers that this is your story.
- Think about what you want to tell your readers.
- Organize your ideas into a beginning, middle, and end.
- Write an interesting introduction that "grabs" your readers.
- Write a conclusion that reflects on the events in your narrative.

Write a personal narrative about something you do well. Use the graphic organizer on page 84 as a guide for writing. Be sure to proofread your writing.

_____

_____

_____

_____

_____

_____

_____

_____

_____

_____

_____

_____

_____

_____

_____

_____

_____

_____

Evaluating a Personal Narrative

Use the chart below to evaluate a personal narrative. Check *Yes* or *No* to answer each question. If the answer is *No*, make notes about ways to revise and improve the narrative.

Question	Yes	No	If No, what needs to be done to improve the narrative?
Does the narrative describe something the writer does well?	✔		
Does the narrative contain a beginning paragraph that captures the reader's attention?			
Does the writer describe how the skill was learned?			
Does the writer explain when the skill is used?			
Does the writer develop the content by adding interesting details?			
Does the writer make the subject interesting by using interesting vocabulary?			
Does the narrative contain an ending paragraph that closes the subject effectively?			
Is the narrative written in first person?			
Does the narrative reveal or suggest the writer's feelings?			
Has the writer corrected mistakes in spelling, grammar, and punctuation?			

Use the notes in the chart and the graphic organizer on page 84 to revise the narrative as needed. Use the information in Units 1–4 to correct grammar, usage, and mechanics problems.

Name _____   Date _____

Personal Narrative: Proofreading

To be a good proofreader, look for one type of error at a time. For example, proofread once for capitalization errors, once for punctuation errors, and once for spelling errors.

PROOFREADER'S MARKS

≡	Capitalize.	∧⊤	Replace something.
⊙	Add a period.	⩗	Transpose.
∧	Add something.	◯	Spell correctly.
⩕	Add a comma.	¶	Indent paragraph.
ⱽⱽ	Add quotation marks.	/	Make a lowercase letter.
ᵧ	Cut something.		

Proofread this excerpt from a personal narrative. Use the proofreader's marks above to correct at least thirteen errors. Pay special attention to paragraph indentations. For misspelled words, write the correct spelling at the bottom of the page.

The first time you're parents leave you at home alone is exciting for every child. I guess. In my case, however, there was a little more excitement than I had anticipated. I was fourteen, my sister Josie was ten, jeannie was seven, kathryn was six, and my brother Messy was just two. Mom and Dad were just going a few miles away to their favorite restaurant. It was their aniversary.

"I'll just tuck Messy into his crib," Mom said. "He'll probably go right to sleep." "Just try to keep things quiet here," added Dad. "We'll be back in about three hours."
I was "in charge," and I felt pretty grown-up about it. The Romeros our next-door neighbors had been breifed by my parents and were watching us carefuly.
That turned out to be a very good thing. My sisters and I were playing checkers when we heard a strange sound. It was a muffled roaring, and it seemed to get louder and louder. Luckily, the Romeros were soon banging on the door, and I was free to panic.
"tornado!" boomed Mr. Romero. We raced to our rooms, threw blankets over our pajamas, grabbed Messy, and dashed to the Romero's basement.

_____

_____

Compare and Contrast Paper

A **compare and contrast paper**

- describes the similarities and differences in two or more items or describes their advantages and disadvantages.

- addresses the same questions about each item.

Analyze this excerpt from a compare and contrast paper. Then, answer the questions.

Jogging is an aerobic exercise that gives your heart and your lungs a good workout. It uses very little special equipment, so it can be practiced at very little expense. Many people like jogging because it gets them out into the fresh air and provides new things to look at, so it's not as boring as some other forms of exercise. On the other hand, some doctors say that joggers can damage their joints with the pounding that jogging gives them. In addition, jogging can be dangerous if traffic is heavy. Besides the possibility of accidents, inhaling car fumes can present problems.

Rowing machines are also good sources of exercise. They provide an aerobic workout that exercises both legs and arms equally, and they also provide a good workout for the heart and lungs. Because people can use their machines indoors, they are not prevented from exercising in bad weather. On the other hand, people with bad knees may have trouble with all the bending involved. Rowing machines are expensive, and some people are bored by the repetitiveness of this form of exercise.

1. What is being compared? _____

   _____

2. Identify four points the writer addresses about each form of exercise.

   _____

   _____

   _____

   _____

3. Summarize the paragraphs by completing the chart below.

HOW JOGGING AND ROWING ARE ALIKE	HOW JOGGING AND ROWING ARE DIFFERENT

Developing the Topic

Good writers use supporting details, such as facts, definitions, concrete details, quotations, or examples, to develop their topic. All details should be relevant, or directly related, to the main idea.

Read the details below. Some would work well to develop a paper comparing and contrasting bobcats and pet cats. Others are not really relevant. Write *relevant* or *irrelevant* to classify each detail.

1. Both bobcats and housecats are basically nocturnal, but many housecats are active during the

   day also. _____

2. Some cities have organizations that rescue homeless cats. _____

3. Bobcats and pet cats are meat-eaters. _____

4. Bobcats are about twice the size of an average-sized housecat. _____

5. The Canada lynx is a larger relative of the bobcat. _____

6. The ancient Egyptians mummified their pet cats when they died. _____

7. Like bobcats and other wild cats, pet cats are excellent hunters. _____

8. Although domestic cats are solitary by nature, they can tolerate one another quite well in

   some situations. _____

Write one relevant piece of information that could be used in a compare and contrast paper on each topic. It can be a fact, a definition, a concrete detail, a quotation, or an example.

9. soccer and hockey _____

   _____

10. graphic novels and short stories _____

   _____

11. hamsters and dogs as pets _____

   _____

12. animated TV shows and regular TV shows _____

   _____

Compare and Contrast Paper: Graphic Organizer

Think about the music you like to listen to. How is it like the music your parents enjoy? How is it different? Plan to write a compare and contrast paper about how the two preferences are alike and different. Use the Venn diagram to help you plan your paper. List what is true only about A in the A circle. List what is true only about B in the B circle. List what is true about both A and B where the two circles overlap.

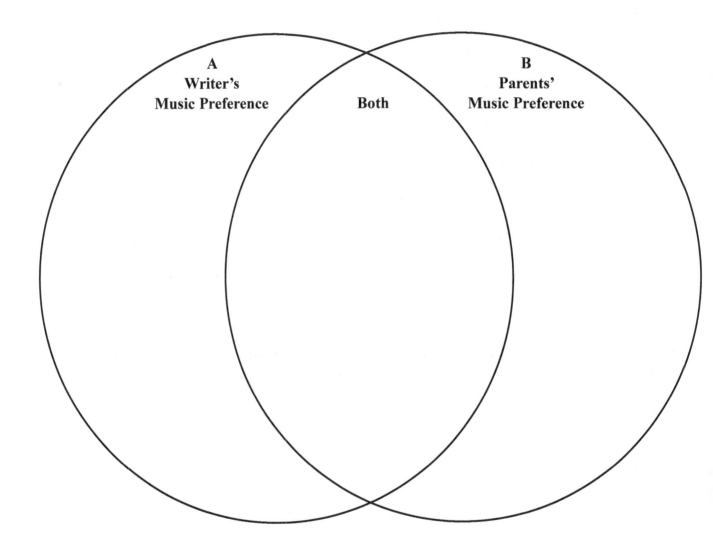

Compare and Contrast Paper: Writing

Tips for Writing a Compare and Contrast Paper
- Find information about your subjects.
- Organize the information you find into main ideas.
- Use details to explain each main idea.
- Explain how the subjects are alike or what advantages they have.
- Explain how the subjects are different or what disadvantages they have.
- Write a concluding statement that follows from the information in your paper.

Compare and contrast the music you like and the music your parents like. Use the Venn Diagram on page 90 as a guide for writing. Be sure to proofread your writing.

_____

_____

_____

_____

_____

_____

_____

_____

_____

_____

_____

_____

_____

_____

_____

_____

_____

_____

_____

_____

Evaluating a Compare and Contrast Paper

Use the chart below to evaluate a compare and contrast paper. Check *Yes* or *No* to answer each question. If the answer is *No*, make notes about ways to revise and improve the paper.

Question	Yes	No	If No, what needs to be done to improve the paper?
Does the writer introduce the subjects for compare/contrast in the first paragraph?	✔		
Does the writer explain how the two subjects are alike?			
Does the writer explain how the two subjects are different?			
Does the writer present more than one idea for each subject?			
Does the writer organize the ideas into paragraphs?			
Does the writer use details to support each point?			
Does the writer summarize the ideas in the paper's conclusion?			
Has the writer corrected mistakes in spelling, grammar, and punctuation?			

Use the notes in the chart and the graphic organizer on page 90 to revise the paper as needed. Use the information in Units 1–4 to correct grammar, usage, and mechanics problems.

Compare and Contrast Paper: Proofreading

To be a good proofreader, look for one type of error at a time. For example, proofread once for capitalization errors, once for punctuation errors, and once for spelling errors.

PROOFREADER'S MARKS

≡ Capitalize.
⊙ Add a period.
∧ Add something.
⩘ Add a comma.
ⱽⱽ Add quotation marks.
⤸ Cut something.

⌒ Replace something.
ᴕ Transpose.
◯ Spell correctly.
⌗ Indent paragraph.
／ Make a lowercase letter.

Proofread this excerpt from a compare and contrast paper. Use the proofreader's marks above to correct at least fourteen errors. Pay special attention to punctuation of sentences. For misspelled words, write the correct spelling at the bottom of the page.

As people's awareness of animal rights has growed, so has the controversy over zoos. Collectors for zoos take animals away from their families and out on their natural habitats. They transport the animals long distances, often under difficult traveling conditions. Zoos are confineing and animals that are placed in them may be prevented from following they're natural instincts. To supply the demand for wild creatures poachers catch some animals illegaly. Certain exotic animals are disappearing from the wild altogether, upsetting the balance of Nature.

On the other hand zoos increase people's awareness of the uniqueness and diversity of the animal population. Many people did'nt begin to care about dolphins, and dolphin safety until they had seen these beautiful, playful animals at zoos or theme parks. Many people now appreciate the importance of the rain forests because they have encountered it's beautiful creatures. It if possible that zoo animals would be more happier in the wild. However, some natural habitats have disappeared so completely that, without the zoo population, many species would now be extinct. Perhaps we need zoos as a refuge.

_____

_____

Descriptive Narrative

> A **descriptive narrative** contains comparisons, descriptive language, and sensory details.

Read the description. Analyze it and answer the questions that follow.

Glad to escape the stale, musty smells in the dive shop, we lumbered outside in our rented dive suits like beached sea turtles. It was still early in the morning, and coiling fingers of steam rolled off the calm water in the cove. We found our boat, huddled among the others. Soon, we were off to find the manatees!

We headed out slowly into the open water, mindful of our wake. Shouting over the din of the motor, we finally agreed to head toward a clump of boats in the distance. As we approached, we scanned the water for telltale bubbles. We all spotted it at once. A manatee was just below the surface ahead on the right! Without a moment's hesitation, two of us jumped over the gunwale into the warm water of Crystal River. We saw before us a large brown "seacow," an apt name for this gentle creature. I had been assured I could touch it, but it was easily four times my size. Gingerly, I reached out and just brushed the manatee's leathery-skinned shoulder with my fingertips. The animal went right on ripping out giant mouthfuls of elodea, or sea grass, just like a living steam shovel. I had touched my first wild sea creature!

1. List a detail from the description that appeals to each of the following senses:

   sight _____

   smell _____

   hearing _____

   touch_____

2. Name two things in the description that are compared to something else. To what are they compared?

   _____

   _____

   _____

3. Underline six phrases in the description that show location.

Using Vivid Language

> Skilled writers use vivid language in their descriptions.

Write three vivid words or phrases a writer might use in place of each common descriptive word. Use a thesaurus if you need help.

1. quiet _____

2. big _____

3. soft _____

4. sour _____

5. red _____

6. cold _____

7. smelly _____

8. nervous _____

9. pale _____

10. thin _____

11. good _____

12. bad _____

13. happy _____

14. sad _____

15. beautiful_____

16. ugly _____

17. fast _____

Rewrite these descriptions of people, using more vivid language.

18. You always know when Rosa enters a room.

_____

19. Jim has an easy way with people.

_____

Descriptive Narrative: Graphic Organizer

Plan to write a descriptive narrative about a trip to any planet in the universe or place in the world. Use the graphic organizer to plan the narrative. Write your subject in the center of the circle. Then, write words that describe the subject or experience on the lines.

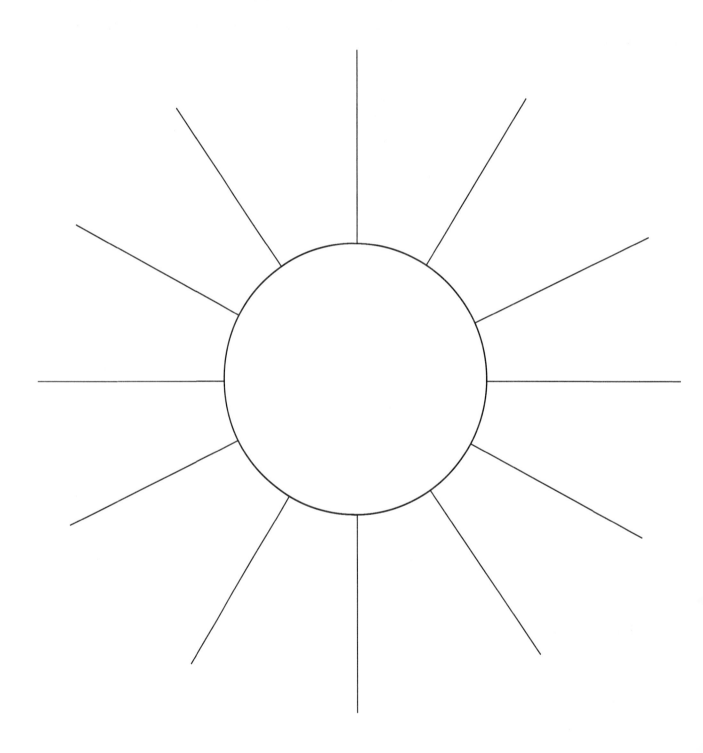

Descriptive Narrative: Writing

Tips for Writing a Descriptive Narrative
- Use your voice when you write. That means you should use your special way of expressing yourself.
- Help readers see, smell, taste, feel, and hear what you are writing about.
- Use vivid words to help you describe.
- Use similes and metaphors to help your readers imagine the experience you are writing about.
- Write a conclusion that wraps up the narrative and supports your descriptions.

Imagine that you could visit any planet in the universe or place in the world. Where would you go and what would you do? Write a descriptive story about your adventure. Use the graphic organizer on page 96 as a guide for writing. Be sure to proofread your writing.

_____

_____

_____

_____

_____

_____

_____

_____

_____

_____

_____

_____

_____

_____

_____

_____

_____

Evaluating a Descriptive Narrative

Use the chart below to evaluate a descriptive narrative. Check *Yes* or *No* to answer each question. If the answer is *No*, make notes about ways to revise and improve the narrative.

Question	Yes	No	If No, what needs to be done to improve the narrative?
Does the writer describe the sights, sounds, smells, tastes, and feel of the experience?	✔		
Does the writer use a unique way of expressing himself or herself?			
Does the writer include vocabulary that is vivid and interesting?			
Does the writer use similes and metaphors to help readers imagine the experience?			
Does the writer use action words to describe what happens?			
Has the writer corrected mistakes in spelling, grammar, and punctuation?			

Use the notes in the chart and the graphic organizer on page 96 to revise the descriptive narrative as needed. Use the information in Units 1–4 to correct grammar, usage, and mechanics problems.

Descriptive Narrative: Proofreading

> To be a good proofreader, look for one type of error at a time. For example, proofread once for capitalization errors, once for punctuation errors, and once for spelling errors.
>
> ## PROOFREADER'S MARKS
>
> | | |
> |---|---|
> | ≡ Capitalize. | ⌃ Replace something. |
> | ⊙ Add a period. | ᶇ Transpose. |
> | ∧ Add something. | ○ Spell correctly. |
> | ⋏ Add a comma. | ⁋ Indent paragraph. |
> | ⌄⌄ Add quotation marks. | / Make a lowercase letter. |
> | ⸐ Cut something. | |

Proofread this excerpt from a descriptive narrative. Use the proofreader's marks above to correct at least thirteen errors. For misspelled words, write the correct spelling at the bottom of the page.

I woke up in the early morning. The planit's three suns, shining through the sides of the tent, created a strange orange glow in the air. It was bitterly cold. I lay in my down sleeping bag, watching my breath frost in front of my eyes. there was not a sound, not a stirring of wind not a bird, not a crack of a twig. It was the kind of quite that made me think of danger, and that was a thought I did not need on this still freezing morning millions miles from home.

I unfurled the stiff, gray cover to the little window in the side of the tent, which I could just reach from the sleeping bag. Outside was a landscape of snow and ice, blue and purple below the sky's dim glow. Heavy straight growths, almost like tree trunks, stuck up out of the snow. None of them had any branches or twigs or, presumably, leafs. We had not even determined weather they were living things.

A low, jagged mountain shimmered in the distance. Crystal mound was it's name. I knew it was formed of strange crystalline shapes of rose, turquoise, and yellow, though its colors looked washed out at this distance. I also knowed that it was growing. We scientists had watched it grow. It was, strangly enough, the only thing on this silent planet that did seem to expand or change.

planet's   quiet   whether   knew   leaves

How-To Paper

A **how-to paper**
- explains a process or procedure.
- introduces the subject in a topic sentence.
- lists the required materials *before* describing the steps.
- precisely states the steps to be taken, in order.

The skillful use of **precise vocabulary** and **time-order words** and phrases is essential in a how-to paper.

Something is missing in each how-to example below. Analyze the examples and identify the missing element. Write it on the line.

1. Changing a flat tire is not difficult. Before you begin, read the instructions about how to use your jack. Loosen the lug nuts while the flat is still on the ground. Then position the jack correctly and jack up the car. Next, unscrew the lugs the rest of the way and remove the flat tire. Replace it with your spare tire. Then screw the lugs as tightly as possible. Finally, release the jack, and you're ready to go!

   _____

2. All you need is an address and a ZIP code directory. First, at a post office, ask to see the directory of ZIP codes. Next, look in the directory for the state your letter is going to. Now, within the state listing, find the city you want. Finally, if it is a large city, you will also have to find the street. The ZIP codes are listed in the right column. Just copy the one you want onto your envelope, and it's ready for the mailbox.

   _____

3. Giving a cat a pill can be difficult. Have these things ready: the pill, a towel, and a friend! Pick up your cat and pet it. Wrap the towel around the cat. Let your friend hold the cat firmly. Put your index fingers and thumbs on a corner of the cat's mouth. Pinch gently until the mouth opens. Place the pill on the back of the cat's tongue. Close the cat's mouth and hold it shut until the cat swallows.

   _____

4. You can make money for your club or organization by having a community bake sale. Compile a list of volunteers to make baked goods, to contact merchants, and to sell the items. Be sure to have a table for displaying the goods, chairs for the cashiers, a metal box for money, and plenty of change. Find a good location.

   _____

Connecting Ideas in Sequence

To write a how-to paragraph, careful writers
- make a "movie" in their minds of the steps involved in the process.
- write the steps in the order in which they "see" them.
- use time-order words to make the sequence clear.
- ensure that the sequence is complete from beginning to end.

The steps below for washing a car are listed out of order. In the diagram, write the steps in the correct order. Add two steps that are missing.

Use window cleaner to clean the windows.
Rinse all soapsuds completely using a garden hose.
Vacuum the inside of the car.
Mix detergent with warm water in a bucket.
Gather all the equipment you will need.
Begin all work at the top of the car and work downward.

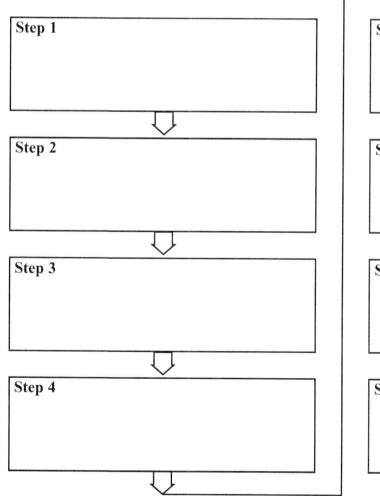

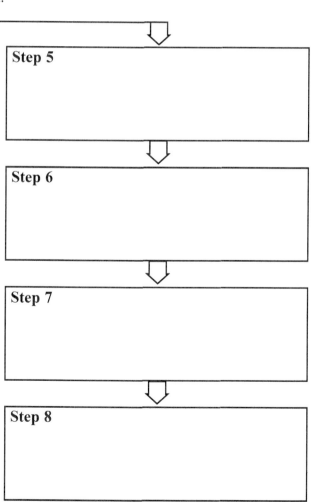

Step 1

Step 2

Step 3

Step 4

Step 5

Step 6

Step 7

Step 8

Using Precise Vocabulary

Skillful writers use precise language to make instructions clear.

Read this how-to paragraph. Rewrite it, replacing vague words with precise words. Make up any amounts and measurements you may need.

Would you like to grow vegetables even though you don't have space in your yard? You can still do it, using containers. Here's how to grow sugar-baby watermelons. Put some dirt into a large tub. Mix in some fertilizer. Also, rig up something for the vines to grow on. Plant the seeds and water them. Place the tub somewhere outside. When the melons are getting heavy, tie them up to the stakes with material so that the weight of the melons won't snap the vines. Sit back and watch your melons grow.

_____

_____

_____

_____

_____

_____

_____

_____

_____

_____

_____

_____

_____

_____

_____

How-To Paper: Graphic Organizer

Think of a task you do often. It may be a job you enjoy or one you dislike. Use the graphic organizer to plan a how-to paper. Adjust the number of steps as needed.

Topic Sentence: _____

Step 1	Step 5

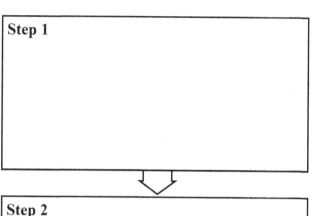
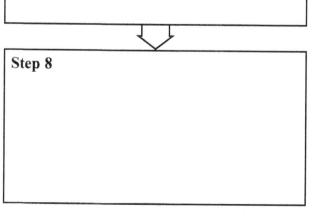

Step 2	Step 6

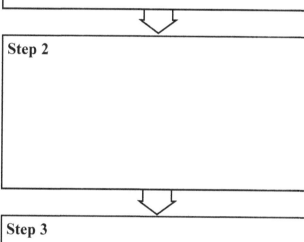

Step 3	Step 7

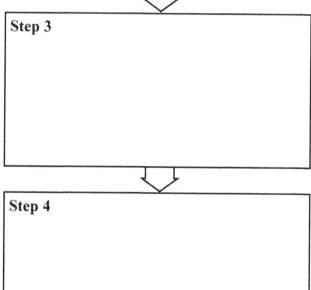

Step 4	Step 8

Name _____ Date _____

How-To Paper: Writing

Tips for Writing a How-To Paper

- Narrow the focus of the process or procedure you choose.

- Be sure the list of materials is complete.

- Be sure you have included every step in the process and that they are in correct sequence.

- Use time-order words as needed.

- Use precise vocabulary throughout the paper. Write an ending that follows naturally from the steps you have explained.

Write a how-to paper describing a task you do often. It may be a job you enjoy or one you dislike. Use the graphic organizer on page 103 as a guide. Proofread your paper carefully.

_____

_____

_____

_____

_____

_____

_____

_____

_____

_____

_____

_____

_____

Evaluating a How-To Paper

Use the chart below to evaluate a how-to paper. Check *Yes* or *No* to answer each question. If the answer is *No*, make notes about ways to revise and improve the paper.

Question	Yes	No	If No, what needs to be done to improve the paper?
Does the writer introduce the subject or problem in a topic sentence?	✔		
Does the writer provide a complete and precise list of the materials required?			
Does the list of materials precede the steps of the process?			
Are the steps presented in order?			
Is the list of steps complete?			
Does the writer use time-order words appropriately?			
Does the writer use precise vocabulary throughout the paper?			
Does the writer seem to be experienced and knowledgeable in performing this task?			
After reading the paper, will readers understand the process or still have questions?			
Has the writer corrected mistakes in spelling, grammar, and punctuation?			

Use the notes in the chart and the graphic organizer on page 103 to revise the paper as needed. Use the information in Units 1–4 to correct grammar, usage, and mechanics problems.

How-To Paper: Proofreading

To be a good proofreader, look for one type of error at a time. For example, proofread once for capitalization errors, once for punctuation errors, and once for spelling errors.

PROOFREADER'S MARKS

≡ Capitalize.
⊙ Add a period.
∧ Add something.
⋏ Add a comma.
ⱽⱽ Add quotation marks.
⤙ Cut something.

⋏ Replace something.
ᴎ Transpose.
◯ Spell correctly.
Ⴤ Indent paragraph.
/ Make a lowercase letter.

Proofread these two excerpts from how-to papers. Use the proofreader's marks above to correct at least thirteen errors. Pay special attention to misspelled words. Write the correct spellings at the bottom of the page.

As the holidays approach, do you dread all those ours you will spend rapping gifts Your worries may be over. Wrapping presents for your family and freinds can be an enjoyable experience if you follow these simple rules. First, by all your wrapping supplies early. Go to a well-stocked paper store and buy these items: gift wrap, ribbon, tape tissue paper, and gift tags. Keep all your wrapping supplies together in one big bag. then wrap as you go. Each time you buy a present, pull out your special bag and wrap the gift. When the write time comes, enjoy giving your beautifully wrapped presents.

Wrapping a package that contains breakibles takes patients and the right wrapping materials. First, find a sturdy box a few inches larger than the object you are mailing. Then buy plastic bubble wrap or foam "peanuts." Suround the object on all sides with padding and be sure it cannot move within the box. Then use strong, touff tape to seal the box. Finally, be sure to write FRAJILE on the box in large clear letters. so everyone who handles your package will know it contains something breakable.

_____

_____

_____

Opinion Essay

An **opinion essay**
- states an opinion or position on an issue.
- provides facts and reasons to support the opinion.
- contains arguments that appeal to the reader's ethics, emotions, or reason.
- has an introductory paragraph, supporting paragraphs, and a conclusion.

Read and analyze this opinion essay. Then, answer the questions.

Should We Kick Out Football?

I am a sports nut. I spend hours glued to the television watching games—hockey, basketball, baseball, and football. I also play on the school's basketball and baseball teams. However, this sports fan has had enough of high school football. At the risk of being shunned by my friends, I say we should kick out football.

If you are growling at me as you read this, let me say that two months ago I would have been on your side. Two months ago, however, I hadn't read my dad's newsletter from the Riverton City Sports Council. The newsletter printed statistics about sports-related injuries in our state's schools. Football causes four hundred times as many injuries as any other sport. Last year, two local players suffered spinal cord injuries. One of those football players is in a wheelchair. He'll never walk again.

Students who play football are taking a terrible chance. One-third of the players sustain some kind of injury during the season. Do you think the new helmets protect players from serious hurt? Wrong! I don't know whether the players are practicing without helmets, or the helmets themselves are inadequate. I do know that 22 student football players in our state suffered head injuries last year. By contrast, only one basketball player in the whole state sustained a head injury.

1. What opinion or position does the writer state in this essay? _____

   _____

2. In what part of the essay does that opinion appear? _____

   _____

3. What type of appeal does the writer use? _____

   _____

   _____

4. Does the essay convince you to agree with the writer's point of view? Why or why not? _____

   _____

   _____

Showing Clear Relationships

Skilled writers use transitional words and phrases to connect ideas and show the relationships between them. In an opinion essay, transitions clarify how the opinion, reasons, and evidence are related.

Write a transitional word or phrase from the chart to complete each sentence. Be sure to show the correct relationship between ideas.

Comparing Ideas	Contrasting Ideas	Showing Cause and Effect	Showing Support
also and another likewise similarly	although but however in spite of instead of	because consequently since so that therefore	for example for instance in fact

Athletes should not charge fans for autographs _____ the fans help many athletes receive huge salaries in the first place. _____, loyal fans pay large amounts for game tickets and buy items such as jerseys and caps. Popular players—the ones fans ask for autographs the most—already make very high salaries. _____, top players make more in a year than most of us will make in a lifetime. Asking fans to pay for autographs, _____, is asking too much. _____ taking our money, athletes should repay our loyalty by freely signing their name to our tattered cards.

Rewrite the passage from an opinion essay using transitional words and phrases. Some sentences can be combined using transitions.

Paper is not very expensive to buy. The environmental cost of making new paper is quite high. We should start a paper-recycling program. A paper-recycling program can help conserve our forests. These forests are worth saving. They are filled with vital oxygen-producing trees. A ton of paper made from recycled material saves approximately seventeen trees. We use about six tons of paper each year at our school. We could potentially save over one hundred trees a year by recycling.

_____

_____

_____

Opinion Essay: Graphic Organizer

Many people think that everyone should learn at least one language other than English. Should students be required to learn a foreign language to graduate from high school? Plan to write an opinion essay expressing your opinion. Use the graphic organizer to help you plan.

What is the topic of your essay?	What is your opinion on this topic?
_____	_____
_____	_____
_____	_____

Reason 1	Why? Support your reason.
_____	_____
_____	_____
_____	_____
	_____

Reason 2	Why? Support your reason.
_____	_____
_____	_____
_____	_____
	_____

Reason 3	Why? Support your reason.
_____	_____
_____	_____
_____	_____
	_____

Opinion Essay: Writing

Tips for Writing an Opinion Essay

- Grab your reader's attention in the first paragraph.
- State your opinion clearly.
- Support your opinion with legitimate arguments and clear examples.
- Present your examples from least important to most important.
- Write a strong conclusion that follows from and supports your argument.

Should students be required to learn a foreign language to graduate from high school? Write an opinion essay expressing your opinion. Use the graphic organizer on page 109 as a guide for writing. Be sure to proofread your writing.

_____

_____

_____

_____

_____

_____

_____

_____

_____

_____

_____

_____

_____

_____

_____

_____

_____

Evaluating an Opinion Essay

Use the chart below to evaluate an opinion essay. Check *Yes* or *No* to answer each question. If the answer is *No*, make notes about ways to revise and improve the essay.

Question	Yes	No	If No, what needs to be done to improve the narrative?
Does the writer state his or her opinion clearly?	✔		
Does the writer grab the reader's attention in the first paragraph?			
Does the writer provide legitimate arguments for the opinion?			
Does the essay include facts, statistics, or examples to support the arguments?			
Does the writer use transitional words and phrases to show the relationships between ideas?			
Does the writer present arguments from least to most important?			
Does the writer appeal to the reader's ethics, emotions, or reason?			
Does the writer summarize his or her position in the last paragraph?			
Does the essay convince the reader of the writer's position?			
Has the writer corrected mistakes in spelling, grammar, and punctuation?			

Use the notes in the chart and the graphic organizer on page 109 to revise the essay as needed. Use the information in Units 1–4 to correct grammar, usage, and mechanics problems.

Opinion Essay: Proofreading

> To be a good proofreader, look for one type of error at a time. For example, proofread once for capitalization errors, once for punctuation errors, and once for spelling errors.
>
> ### PROOFREADER'S MARKS
>
> | | |
> |---|---|
> | ☰ Capitalize. | ⌃ Replace something. |
> | ⊙ Add a period. | ⁊ Transpose. |
> | ∧ Add something. | ○ Spell correctly. |
> | ⋏ Add a comma. | ⁋ Indent paragraph. |
> | ⌄⌄ Add quotation marks. | / Make a lowercase letter. |
> | ⌙ Cut something. | |

Proofread this excerpt from an opinion essay. Use the proofreader's marks above to correct at least fourteen errors. Pay special attention to capitalization of proper nouns. For misspelled words, write the correct spelling at the bottom of the page.

The people of the World are faced with alarming environmental problems. I am convinced that we must all cooperate through international agencys to solve these problems. Working alone, one state or or one nation cannot protect its land and people from environmental hazzards. The problems faced by people in the united states are also problems for people in canada, Japan, and russia. Only by facing these problems together and trying to work out cooperative solutions can we protect ourselves and our Planet.

International cooperation is needed for several reasons. in the first place, some environmental dangers threaten the whole planet rather than local areas. Damage to the ozone layer is a good example. If someone in Nebraska uses an aerosol spray, the chemicals do not stay in Nebraska. Those damaging chemicals travel to the ozone layer, where they effect the hole world. Therefore, a State or Country cannot protect itself against ozone damage simply by passing a law forbiding the local use of aerosols.

_____

_____

Capturing the Reader's Interest

> Skilled writers capture the reader's interest by
> - creating a good title.
> - using a catchy beginning.
> - creating a satisfying ending.

Circle the letter of the best title for a personal narrative. Write a sentence explaining why you think that title is best.

1. **a.** My First Day of School
   b. How I Broke My Leg (and Put My Foot in My Mouth)
   c. August 27, 2013

   _____

2. **a.** Terror!
   b. My Most Frightening Experience
   c. How I Escaped from the Leopard

   _____

3. **a.** The School Play
   b. Starring Harry Lee as an Oak Tree!
   c. My First Part in a Play

   _____

Put a check mark next to the story beginning with the better "hook." Write a sentence explaining why you chose it.

4. _____ This was going to be the end of life as I knew it. What a mistake!

   _____ I made a big mistake when I was 12 years old.

   _____

   _____

5. _____ Did you ever wake up just knowing something special was about to happen?

   _____ When I woke up, I knew it would be a special day.

   _____

   _____

Varying Sentence Length

Careful writers vary the length of their sentences by
- avoiding too many short, choppy sentences.
- avoiding too many long, complicated sentences.
- combining choppy sentences to make longer, smoother sentences.
- shortening or dividing long, complicated sentences.

Rewrite this paragraph. Combine short, choppy sentences to create a smooth writing style, and divide sentences that are too long or complex.

Last week, I came to your store. I bought an exercise bike. The sales clerk informed me that delivery would be made within seven days. Seven days passed. No delivery was made. I called customer service. Because I had kept the receipt from the week before, I was able to give the customer service people the invoice number of the sale, and they, in turn, were able to trace the record of the sale, which was still in the sporting goods department. Then I talked with the manager of sporting goods. He told me that the store does not deliver to my town. I am angry.

_____

_____

_____

_____

_____

_____

_____

_____

_____

_____

_____

_____

Using Formal and Informal Language

Skillful writers change their writing to use

• an appropriately formal and serious tone in research reports and other formal compositions.

• an informal and casual tone in less serious writing.

Write *formal* or *informal* to identify the language in each sentence. Then, rewrite the sentence. If it is formal writing, make it informal. If it is informal, make it formal.

1. Carnivorous plants use an unorthodox method of obtaining nutrients.

   _____

   _____

2. They trap insects inside specially constructed plant structures, which then secrete digestive juices.

   _____

   _____

3. Since these plants are incapable of stalking their prey, they have developed snares.

   _____

   _____

4. Sundews have leaves that are sort of like little spoons, with sticky hairs on the edges.

   _____

   _____

5. Teeny flying bugs use the hairs as a landing field, and they can get stuck forever on these gooey surfaces.

   _____

   _____

6. Butterworts' leaves practically drip "butter," gooey stuff that's great for catching bugs.

   _____

   _____

Unit 6: Research Skills
Kinds of Books

The library has different kinds of books. The book groups are usually housed in separate sections or rooms in the library.

Fiction books include novels and short stories.

Nonfiction books tell facts about real people, things, or events. A **biography** is a nonfiction book that tells about the life of a real person.

A **periodical** is a published work that appears in a series. Newspapers and magazines are periodicals.

Reference books, such as encyclopedias, dictionaries, and thesauruses, are good sources of information on many subjects.

Write *fiction, nonfiction, biography, periodical,* or *reference* to identify the type of book described in each question.

1. the novel *Maniac Magee* _____

2. the *Merriam-Webster Dictionary* _____

3. a book about the history of the National Park Service _____

4. an encyclopedia article about Camp David _____

5. a magazine from the American Camping Association _____

6. maps of camping areas in your state _____

7. a book titled *Scary Stories from Around the Campfire* _____

8. a book titled *The Synonym Finder* _____

9. a book titled *How to Set Up a Campsite* _____

10. a book titled *Bartlett's Familiar Quotations* _____

11. a newspaper article about summer camps _____

12. a book that tells about the life of Juliette Low _____

13. the book *Harry Potter and the Sorcerer's Stone* _____

14. a book titled *Information Please Almanac* _____

15. a book titled *Lincoln: A Photobiography* _____

The Parts of a Book

The **title page** tells the name of the book, its author, and the name of the company that published the book.

The **copyright page** is on the back of the title page. It tells when the book was published.

The **acknowledgments page** names those who helped develop the book's content. It officially recognizes the contributions made by sources other than the author.

The **foreword/preface** contains introductory comments about the book. It can be written by the author or someone else.

The **contents page** lists the titles of the chapters or units in the book and the pages on which they begin.

The **glossary** contains definitions of difficult or unfamiliar words that appear in the book.

The **bibliography** is a list of books about a certain subject. It can also be a list of books the author used or referred to in the text.

The **index** is a list of all the topics in a book. It is in alphabetical order and lists the page or pages on which each topic appears.

Identify the part of a book where the following information can be found.

1. To find the meaning of a technical term used in a book, you would look in the _____.

2. If you want to do further reading about a subject, you would consult the book's _____.

3. You want to know if the book you are reading is up-to-date. To find out when the book was published, you would look on the _____.

4. A friend hands you a book called *Back to My Roots*, and you wonder if Alex Haley is the author. Where in the book would you look? _____

5. You want to know who helped Alex Haley research his story. To find out, you would read the

   _____.

6. You are researching the history of Gambia, but the *Encyclopedia of World History* doesn't have a chapter on that country. Where else in the book would you look to see if Gambia is in the book?

   _____.

7. Where would you find the name of a book's publisher? _____

8. You are looking for books about life in traditional African villages in the 1700s. The librarian hands you a stack of books. Where would you look first to select books that suit your purpose?

   _____

Using a Table of Contents

A **table of contents** lists the titles of the chapters or units in a book and gives the pages on which they begin. Contents pages can help readers examine the subjects covered in a book.

Read this table of contents for a science book about oceans. Answer the questions that follow.

CONTENTS

Chapter 1   Along the Shore 1
Chapter 2   Life Among the Coral Reefs 23
Chapter 3   Life in the Depths 55
Chapter 4   Ocean Mammals 79
Chapter 5   Sea Birds 117
Chapter 6   Ocean Resources 135
Chapter 7   Our Oceans in Danger 159
Glossary 171

1. In which chapter would you find information about whales, dolphins, and sea otters? _____

   How do you know? _____

2. In which chapter would you expect to find pictures of the damage caused by an oil slick? _____

   What makes you think so? _____

3. Which is the longest chapter? _____

4. In which chapter might you find out how coral reefs are formed? _____

5. You're interested in finding out what kinds of seaweed grow near coastlines. Where would you

   look? _____

6. You want to find out what the word *salinity* means. Where might you find it in this book?

   _____

7. In which chapter might you find information about pelicans? _____

8. You want to learn which creatures live in the deepest parts of the ocean. Which chapter would you

   read? _____

9. Which is the shortest chapter? _____

10. In which chapter would you find out what valuable things we can get from the oceans? _____

Using an Index

Many nonfiction books and most encyclopedias have an **index** of subject titles, listed in alphabetical order. The index shows the volume and the page number where an article can be found. Some encyclopedias contain articles on many different topics. Other encyclopedias contain different articles relating to a broad topic.

Use the sample encyclopedia index to answer the questions below.

Index
Acorn Squash, 1–6; **11**–1759
        Baked, supreme, **1**–7
        Steamed, **1**–7
Appetizer(s), **1**–84; *see also* Dip; Pickle and Relish; Spread
        Almonds, **1**–89
        Celery, stuffed, **1**–89
        Cheese Ball, **3**–429
Cabbage, **2**–256; *see also* Salads, Coleslaw; Sauerkraut
        with bacon and cheese sauce, **1**–68
Flour, **5**–705
        Peanut, **8**–1328
        Rice, **10**–1556
        Wheat, **12**–1935

1. In what volume would you find an article on stuffed celery? _____

2. On what page would you find information on cabbage with bacon and cheese sauce? _____

3. Are all articles on flour found in the same volume? _____

4. What are the cross-references for **Appetizer(s)**? _____

_____

5. Do the words in bold show the name of the volume or the name of the main food or ingredient?

_____

6. Which main food or ingredient has articles in two volumes? _____

7. Information on which appetizers can be found in the same volume and on the same page? _____

_____

8. What main ingredient is found in Volume 5? _____

9. If you looked under **Dip**, what might you expect to find as a cross-reference? _____

Using a Dictionary

A **dictionary** lists words in alphabetical order, giving their pronunciation, part of speech, and definition. Each word in the dictionary is called an **entry word**. Two **guide words** are located at the top of every dictionary page. The word on the left is the first entry word on that page, and the word on the right is the last entry word.

Read the dictionary entries and answer the questions that follow.

nation   **nature**

na·tion [nā′shən] *n.* **1** A group of people who live in a particular area, have a distinctive way of life, and are organized under a central government. They usually speak the same language. **2** *n.* A tribe or federation: the Iroquois *nation.*
na·tion·al [nash′ən·əl] **1** *adj.* Of, belonging to, or having to do with a nation as a whole: A *national* law; a *national* crisis. **2** *n.* a citizen of a nation. **–na′tion·al·ly** *adv.*
na·tion·wide [nā′shən·wīd′] *adj.* Extending throughout or across a nation.

na·tive [nā′tiv] **1** *adj.* Born, grown, or living naturally in a particular area. **2** *n.* A person, plant, or animal native to an area. **3** *n.* One of the original inhabitants of a place; aborigine. **4** *adj.* Related or belonging to a person by birth or place of birth: one's *native* language.
Native American One of or a descendant of the peoples living in the Western Hemisphere before the first Europeans came.
na·tive-born [nā′tiv-bôrn′] *adj.* Born in the area or country stated: a *native-born* Floridian.

1. What part of speech is *nation*? _____

2. What part of speech is *native-born*? _____

3. What is the meaning of *nationwide*? _____

   _____

4. What is the base word of *nationally*? _____

5. Which meaning of the word *nation* is used in the following sentence?

   Wilma Mankiller was the first woman to become chief of the Cherokee *nation.*

   _____

6. What is the entry word for *nationally*? _____

7. How many syllables does *nationwide* have? _____

8. Would *natural* be found on the page with the guide words shown above? _____

Using a Thesaurus

A **thesaurus** is a book that gives synonyms, words that have nearly the same meaning, and antonyms, words that mean the opposite of a word. Many thesauruses are like dictionaries. The entry words are listed in dark print in alphabetical order. Guide words at the top of the page tell which words can be found on the page. Use a thesaurus to enrich your vocabulary and make your writing more colorful.

Rewrite each sentence. Use a thesaurus to replace the underlined word.

1. Henry's heart <u>beat</u> as the ship pushed forward.

   _____

2. The waves <u>grew</u> higher while the ship turned toward the storm, as if to meet it head-on.

   _____

3. Henry's first voyage as a working sailor was already more <u>exciting</u> than his wildest dreams.

   _____

4. The black clouds <u>hung</u> overhead, but the captain seemed to ignore them.

   _____

5. The wind <u>blew</u> against the sails and plunged the ship in and out of foaming white water.

   _____

6. A cold chill reached Henry's skin from deep inside his stomach, as his excitement turned to <u>fear</u>.

   _____

7. High up on the ship's bridge, the <u>experienced</u> captain looked down at the crew working on the deck.

   _____

8. <u>Seeing</u> the look of fear on young Henry's face, the captain suddenly descended to the deck.

   _____

9. He wanted to <u>tell</u> the crew that the storm would soon pass and the sea would become calm once again.

   _____

10. But who can really soothe an inexperienced sailor who is about to <u>face</u> his first raging storm?

   _____

121

Using an Encyclopedia

An **encyclopedia** is a set of reference books, each of which is called a **volume**. Each volume contains many articles on various topics. The topics are arranged alphabetically, and the spine of each volume indicates which articles are within. For example, a spine that is labeled *N-O* indicates that the volume has articles beginning with the letters *N* and *O*. At the end of most articles, related topics are listed. These listed items are called **cross-references**. Often you can find more information about your topic in these articles.

Read the entry for *armadillo* in an encyclopedia and answer the following questions.

1. Where do armadillos live? _____

2. What do they eat? _____

3. How do they protect themselves? _____

4. How much do they weigh? _____

Read the entry for *Sir Edmund Hillary* in an encyclopedia and answer the following questions.

5. Why is Sir Edmund Hillary famous? _____

6. What country was he from? _____

7. How did Hillary originally earn his living? _____

8. How high is Mount Everest? _____

Read the entry for *Zimbabwe* in an encyclopedia and answer the following questions.

9. Where is Zimbabwe located? _____

10. Does it have a coast? _____

11. What is the former name of Zimbabwe? _____

12. What are the most important agricultural products? _____

Read the entry for *rice* in an encyclopedia and answer the following questions.

13. Why is rice an important food crop? _____

14. Where is 90% of the world's rice grown? _____

15. How is most rice grown in Asia? _____

16. Where is the most rice eaten? _____

Using an Atlas

An **atlas** is a book of maps. The maps, charts, and text report the size, population, climate, rainfall, and natural resources of a region. A **map legend** shows what the symbols on the map represent. A **compass rose** tells where north, south, east, and west are on the map. Some compass roses include the intermediate directions (NW, SW, NE, SE).

Use an atlas of the United States to answer these questions about Tennessee.

1. What is the capital of Tennessee? _____

2. How many states border Tennessee? _____

   Which state lies on Tennessee's eastern border? _____

3. How many people live in Tennessee? _____

4. What national park is in Tennessee? _____

5. What interstate highway crosses the state from east to west? _____

6. In which direction would you travel to go from Knoxville to Nashville? _____

7. What mountain range is in Tennessee? _____

8. How much money does the average household in Tennessee earn per year? _____

Use a world atlas to answer these questions about Switzerland.

9. In what part of Europe is Switzerland located? _____

10. Is the country inland? _____ If not, which body of water borders it? _____

11. Name the countries that border Switzerland. _____

12. Which rivers run through Switzerland? _____

13. What is the capital of Switzerland? _____

14. What mountain range is in Switzerland? _____

15. What kind of climate does Switzerland have? _____

16. What languages do the people in Switzerland speak? _____

_____

Using an Almanac

An **almanac** is a reference book that is published yearly. Almanacs give information on many topics of interest, such as weather forecasts, tides, times of sunrises, and astronomy. Often the information in almanacs is provided in tables, graphs, and statistics.

Almanacs also contain articles on people who have made news during the past year. As an extra feature, almanacs often include lists of noteworthy people and events over a period of time. The subject matter of the lists varies from year to year.

Use the information below from an almanac to answer the questions.

Noted Aviators Through the Ages

Leonardo da Vinci	Italy 1452–1519
Jean P. Blanchard	France 1753–1809
the Montgolfier brothers	France 1740–1810
Salomon A. Andrée	Sweden 1854–1897
the Wright brothers	United States 1867–1948
Louis Blériot	France 1872–1936
Blanche S. Scott	United States 1892–1970
Amelia Earhart	United States 1897–1937 (?)
Charles A. Lindbergh	United States 1902–1974
Jacqueline Cochran	United States 1910–1980

1. Which noted aviator lived before the 1700s? _____

2. Which two countries have the greatest number of aviators listed? _____

_____

3. Which noted aviators lived into the twentieth century? _____

_____

4. Which noted aviators lived in only one century? _____

_____

5. According to this almanac, which country dominated aviation during the twentieth century?

_____

6. Which countries are represented only once in this list? _____

7. Which aviator's year of death is not known for certain? _____

Using References to Find Information

> **atlas**—a book of maps
>
> **thesaurus**—a book of synonyms and antonyms
>
> **dictionary**—a book that gives the pronunciations and definitions of words
>
> **almanac**—a book that is published each year and gives facts about various topics such as the tides, weather, and the time the sun rises. Much of the information is presented in charts, tables, and graphs. An almanac also presents general information.
>
> **encyclopedia**—a set of volumes that has articles about various topics
>
> *Books in Print*—a book that lists books that have been published about various subjects

Write the correct reference source for each item of information. Choose from the list below. There may be more than one correct answer.

> atlas   almanac   thesaurus   encyclopedia   dictionary   *Books in Print*

1. **Languages** — It is estimated that there are thousands of languages spoken in the world. Following is a list of the major languages spoken by the greatest number of people. They are ranked in order of usage.

Name of Language	Major Areas Where Spoken
Chinese (Mandarin)	China
English (has the most words – 790,000)	U.S., U.K., Canada, Ireland, Australia, New Zealand

   _____

2. **sincere** — honest, truthful, honorable, frank, open, aboveboard, unreserved, veracious, true, candid

   _____

3. **writing** — visible recording of language peculiar to the human species. Writing permits the transmission of ideas over vast distances of time and space and is essential to complex civilization. The first known writing dates from 6000 B.C.

   _____

4. **language** [lang´ gwij] *n.* **1. a.** Spoken or written human speech. *Language* is used to communicate thoughts and feelings. **b.** A particular system of human speech that is shared by a group of people. **2.** Any system of signs, symbols, or gestures used for giving information.

   _____

5. books about soccer

   _____

Name _____ Date _____

The Dewey Decimal System

The **Dewey Decimal System** was published by Melvil Dewey in 1876 and is still used in most school libraries today. The DDS is a way to classify **nonfiction** books by dividing them into ten broad categories. The categories are organized as follows:

000–099 General reference books	500–599 Pure sciences
100–199 Philosophy	600–699 Technology
200–299 Religion	700–799 Arts and recreation
300–399 Social sciences	800–899 Literature
400–499 Linguistics/language	900–999 General geography and history

Answer the questions using the Dewey Decimal System chart above.

1. Michael needs to find the words to some popular rock songs. In which section will he probably find books of lyrics? _____

2. Where should Erica look for information about the religions of India? _____

3. Mario is doing a report on the differences in the pronunciation of Spanish in Puerto Rico, Cuba, and Mexico City. Where should he look? _____

4. Hoda wants to find out why certain speakers have better sound than others. Which section will probably have the information she needs? _____

5. Jasmine needs a copy of *The Historical Atlas of the 20th Century* to find information about the break-up of the British Empire. Where will she find the atlas? _____

6. Thieu wants to find a copy of Gary Paulsen's novel *Hatchet*. Which section contains the information he wants? _____

Write book titles or make up imaginary book titles that would be found under each of the following DDS classifications.

7. 300–399: _____

8. 500–599: _____

9. 700–799: _____

10. 900–999: _____

Using Text Divisions and Emphasis

> When you are reading for specific information, you will succeed more easily if you learn to use text divisions and emphasis tools. Important words often appear in **boldface** type, *italics*, or CAPS. **Subheads** and **marginal labels** help readers understand how the information is organized. They also help readers locate information more quickly.

Answer the questions.

1. In a science textbook, which word in the following paragraph might you expect to find in boldface print or italics? Why?

    Ice in the form of glaciers can change the shape of the land. Glaciers are large sheets of ice. As they move across the land, they pick up rocks and soil. Glaciers can carve valleys into the land and make hills level.

    _____

2. In a science textbook, under which of the following subheads would you most likely find information about how waves change the shape of the land?

    Ice Changes Land

    Waves

    From Rain to Rivers

    _____

3. Write the question answered by these sentences from a social studies textbook.

    One reason Cuban Americans have been successful is their tradition of helping one another. For example, some of the first Cubans who came to the United States were wealthy professionals who were able to start their own businesses. These businesspeople gave many jobs to the Cubans who came later.

    _____

4. In a science textbook, which words in the following paragraph might you expect to find in boldface type or italics? Why?

    In the human body, the circulatory system serves as a delivery system. The blood vessels are like canals carrying supplies everywhere. Some blood vessels are large and some are very small. They carry nutrients to every part of the body.

    _____

Adjusting Reading Rates

Students use different reading strategies depending on the type of material they are reading and their purpose for reading it. Readers use a **relaxed rate** when reading for pleasure. **Skimming** means looking over a book or reference source quickly to identify its subject and find out how it is organized. **Scanning** means looking quickly through a passage to find key words or phrases. Scanning is a fast way to locate specific information.

Read the selections and answer the questions.

porcine [pôr sin] *adj.* of, relating to, or suggesting swine, pigs, or hogs.

Amanda was not expecting a pig as a pet. A cat, a dog, even a gerbil would have seemed better suited to her family's suburban home. The pig had turned up unannounced, unsolicited, and unfed at her very doorstep. No one knew where it came from or to whom it belonged. It was a homeless pig. There were already too many "uns" in this pig's life. Amanda wasn't going to let it be unloved as well.

HOG A mature specimen of the family Suidae, raised extensively in most areas of the world for food. These cloven-hoofed animals have round bodies and short legs and are also referred to as pigs or swine. Domestic breeds include the Chester White, Berkshire, Spotted Poland, Chine, and Yorkshire.

1. How would you read a piece to skim for information? _____

   _____

2. How would you read a piece to scan for information? _____

   _____

3. Which of these selections would you scan? _____

   _____

4. Which selection might you read at a relaxed rate? _____

   _____

5. How would you read the dictionary entry to prepare for a vocabulary test? _____

   _____

6. Which selection might you read slowly, taking notes as you read? Why might you do this?

   _____

   _____

Taking Notes

Taking notes helps you organize information when you do research. Some facts are more important than others. Write down only the main ideas when you take notes.

Read the following paragraphs and take notes about them on the note cards below.

Among women in history, Queen Hatshepsut of Egypt holds a special place. She was the only woman ever to rule Egypt with the all-powerful title of pharaoh. Hatshepsut succeeded her husband Thutmose II to the throne about 1504 B.C. She enjoyed a relatively long reign, ruling as pharaoh for twenty-one years. During that time, Hatshepsut was remarkably productive. Egypt's trade improved under her leadership, and she embarked on a major building program.

NOTES

_____

_____

_____

_____

Meng T'ien, the general in charge of building the Great Wall, is also credited with another, smaller construction project. Sometime before 200 B.C., General T'ien is believed to have invented the *cheng*, a musical instrument of the zither family. Like other zithers of Asia, the *cheng* has a long, slightly curved sound box with strings that stretch the length of the instrument. Frets, or stops, are located on the sound box to help produce the melody. Although the *cheng* is no longer popular in China, its descendants are still popular in other Asian countries. In Vietnam, the *tranh* is still used for courtly music, and the *koto* enjoys wide popularity in Japan.

NOTES

_____

_____

_____

_____

Outlines

An **outline** organizes information into main topics, subtopics, and details. An outline follows certain rules of capitalization and punctuation.

Write *main topic*, *subtopic*, or *detail* to identify each item in this part of an outline.

I. Loch Ness monster _____

   A. Where it lives _____

      1. Northern Scotland _____

      2. Deep, narrow lake _____

   B. What it looks like _____

      1. Small head _____

      2. Long, thin neck _____

      3. Body 90 feet long _____

The information in this outline is in the correct order. Find the error or errors in each line, and write the line correctly. Remember to indent the lines properly.

II. the Yeti _____

   a. where it lives _____

      1. in Asia _____

      2. in the Himalayas _____

   b. what it looks like _____

      1. large ape or man _____

      2. covered with hair _____

Research famous monsters or other imaginary creatures. Write an outline of the information you find. Revise and proofread your work, checking for correct outline form.

Answer Key

page 1
1. common: mysteries, kinds, books; proper: Uncle Harry,
2. common: night; proper: *The Hound of the Baskervilles*,
3. common: tale; proper: Sir Arthur Conan Doyle,
4. common: character; proper: Doyle, Sherlock Holmes,
5. common: class, book; proper: *Encyclopedia Brown Carries On*, 6–7. Sentences will vary. Possible short answers: 6. game, 7. activist, 8–9. Short answers and sentences will vary.

page 2
1. Flocks, 2. groups, 3. committee, 4. collection, 5. classes, 6. crowd, 7–9. Sentences will vary. 10. bread, 11. jelly, 12. pollen, 13. dust, 14–15. Sentences will vary.

page 3
1. they; trappers, 2. him; Pierre Dorion, 3. they; sons, 4. it; snowstorm, 5. they; boys, 6. him; singular, masculine; her; singular, feminine, 7. them; plural, neuter, 8. I; singular, feminine; them; plural, neuter

page 4
1. she; subject, 2. her; object, 3. its; possessive, 4. she; subject, 5. they; subject, 6. them; object, 7. We; subject, 8. Her; possessive, 9. subject, 10. possessive, 11. object, 9–11. Sentences will vary.

page 5
1. These; demonstrative, 2. herself; reflexive, 3. Everyone; indefinite, 4. Which; interrogative, 5. everything; indefinite, 6. each; indefinite, 7. That; demonstrative, 8. herself; reflexive, 9. What; interrogative, 10. No one; indefinite

page 6
1. struggle; action, 2. seem; linking, 3. grunt; action, wallow; action, 4. are; linking, 5. adores; action, 6. brought; action, 7. cruised; action, oinked; action, 8. ate; action, 9. looked; linking, 10. seemed; linking, 11. linking, 12. action, 11–12. Sentences will vary.

page 7
1. main: know; helping: may, 2. main: haunt; helping: do, 3. main: help; helping: can, 4. main: helped; helping: have, 5. main: know; helping: might, 6. main: dictated; helping: had, Possible answers: 7. could, 8. would

page 8
1. act; present, 2. will practice; future, 3. memorize, test; present, 4. invited; past, 5. created; past, will direct; future, 6. adds; present, 7. will face; future, 8. field; present; lost, past, 9. pitched; past, will be; future, 10. will replace; future, 11–14. Answers will vary.

page 9
1. has painted, 2. had developed, 3. have existed, 4. has achieved, 5. had carried, 6. has improved, 7. will have earned, 8. had started

page 10
1. was; intransitive, 2. lived; intransitive, 3. loved; transitive, 4. showed; transitive, 5. died; intransitive, 6. gave; transitive, 7. was; intransitive, 8. stopped, stared; intransitive, 9. had found; transitive, 10. brought; transitive, 11. told; transitive, 12. gave; transitive, 13–14. Answers will vary.

page 11
1. jog, 2. have raced, 3. are following, 4. extends, 5. commemorates, 6. had started, 7. threatened, 8. carried, 9. are trying

page 12
1. taken, 2. known, 3. gotten, 4. grown, 5. worn, 6. rode, 7. chose, 8. froze, 9. Celia has come to the family reunion for five years. 10. Her friend brought her this year because she had a broken arm. 11. Paolo drove up to the entrance in a big black car.

page 13
1. adjectives: powerful, sociable; nouns: lion, creature, 2. adjectives: mischievous, important, watchful; nouns: cubs, skills, adults, 3. adjectives: ancient, grassy; nouns: times, areas, 4. adjective: small; noun: number, 5. proper adjectives: British, Mediterranean; articles: A, a, the, 6. proper adjective: English; common adjective: most; article: the, 7. proper adjective: African; common adjective: fascinating; articles: The, the, 8. proper adjective: Egyptian; common adjective: unforgettable; articles: the, an, 9. Sentences will vary.

page 14
1. Those; pronoun; 2. This; adjective, 3. These; adjective, 4. This; pronoun, 1–4. Sentences will vary. 5. N, 6. V, 7. V, 8. A

page 15
1. stranger; comparative, 2. reliable; positive, 3. weirdest; superlative, 4. longer; comparative, 5. most amazing; superlative

page 16
1. firmly; believe; how, 2. completely; have changed; to what extent, 3. overhead; are being sighted; where, 4. sometimes; fool; when, 5. never; will be convinced; how often or when, 6. arrive; verb, 7. likely; adjective, 8. watch; verb, 9. dangerous; adjective, 10. loudly; adverb, 11. warned; verb, 12. careless; adjective, 13. observe; verb

page 17
1. positive, 2. superlative, 3. comparative, 4. positive, 5. comparative, 6. comparative, 7. superlative, 8–10. Answers will vary. Possible answers: 8. deeply, 9. better, 10. more

page 18

1. strange; adjective, 2. strangely; adverb, 3. unusual; adjective, 4. unusually; adverb, 5. immense; adjective, 6. immensely; adverb, 7. well; adverb, 8. good; adjective

page 19

1. by, 2. without, 3. through, 4. in, 5. at, 6. in an office building; during one year, 7. with pillows; under their feet, 8. of milk; in a lifetime, 9. over the railings; of the large ship, 10. down the gangplank; onto the dock, 11. beneath an overcast sky; into the cold Atlantic Ocean, 12. among the strangers; about her new life

page 20

1. with long tails; hats, 2. of spiders; relatives, 3. of the horseshoe crab; mouth, 4. underneath the crab's body; opening, 5. on Earth; live, 6. with great intelligence; behave, 7. through its lungs; must breathe, 8. for long periods; can dive, 9. from the moon; ADJ, 10. by the Apollo space mission; ADV, 11. on the lunar equator; ADJ, 12. by a star's complete collapse; ADV, 13. from space; ADJ, 14. by a falling meteorite; ADV

page 21

1. neither, nor; correlative, 2. and; coordinating, 3. but; coordinating, 4. and, coordinating, 5. or; coordinating, 6. but, coordinating, 7. either, or; correlative, 8. and; coordinating, 9. Llamas are quite affectionate, and they enjoy humans as company. 10. Llamas have no natural defenses like horns, but they spit to show they are mad. 11. Llamas are tamer than farm animals, so they make good pets. 12. You can check out a book about llamas, or you can research them on the Internet.

page 22

1. If, 2. because, 3. since, 4. Although, 5. When, 6. after, 7–10. Answers may vary. Possible answers: 7. Frank agreed to paint several rooms because he needed the money. 8. He knew the work would be dirty and exhausting; however, the price was right. 9. Frank scrubbed hard for two hours; consequently, the walls were free of dirt. 10. The paint on one wall was thin; still, he never would have noticed something beneath the surface.

page 23

1. Say, you're not superstitious, are you? 2. Really, no one believes in that silly stuff anymore. 3. Ouch! I broke a mirror and cut my finger. 4. Oh, no! Some people believe that's seven years' bad luck. 5. Hey, we thought you didn't believe in superstitions. 6. Oops! Well, it doesn't hurt to be careful. 7–15. Answers will vary.

page 24

1. to work in my garden, 2. to plant my garden, 3. to attract hummingbirds, 4. to grow here, 5. object, 6. infinitive, 7. object, 8. modifier, 9–11. Answers will vary.

page 25

1. Running long distances, 2. jogging about three miles per day, 3. Giving in to aches and pains, 4. reciting a favorite poem, 5. Refusing to quit, 6. gerund, 7. modifier, 8. modifier, 9. gerund, 10. object, 11. subject, 12. object of preposition, 13. direct object, 14. object of preposition, 15. subject

page 26

1. living in the mountains; Josh, 2. perched on tree limbs; birds, 3. scampering around briskly; chipmunks, 4. worn from use; field guide, 5. modifier, 6. participle, 7. participle, 8. object, 9–10. Sentences will vary. 9. protecting, 10. written

page 27

1. complete, 2. incomplete, 3. complete, 4. incomplete, 5. complete, 6. complete, 7. incomplete, 8–10. Answers will vary. 11. natural, 12. inverted, 13. natural, 14. inverted, 15. natural

page 28

1. period; imperative, 2. question mark; interrogative, 3. exclamation point; exclamatory, 4. period; declarative, 5. exclamation point; exclamatory, 6. period; imperative, 7. question mark; interrogative, 8. period; declarative, 9. Is a llama a wild animal? 10. Research the various habitats of the llama. 11. Llamas have only two toes on each foot.

page 29

1. A wooden feeder for the birds; feeder, 2. The clear, pleasant whistles of the goldfinches; whistles, 3. Our chubby orange kitty; kitty, 4. She; She, 5. I; I, 6. *Birds of North America*; *Birds of North America*, 7. A strong telescope; telescope, 8. Even relatively small binoculars; binoculars, 9. Myon and I; went, 10. Myon and his dad; took, 11. Myon, his dad, or I; should have thought, 12. We and all our equipment; were soaked, 13. Our sleeping bags and down jackets; looked, 14. Myon and I; were

page 30

1. put the new plants on the ground; put, 2. dug a separate hole for each plant; dug, 3. watered the plants generously; watered, 4. sprouted soon on all the plants; sprouted, 5. were growing well; were growing, 6. had bloomed, though; had bloomed, 7. inspected the garden one morning; inspected, 8. had suddenly produced three lovely flowers; had produced, 9. came out of the house and sat on the porch; Alfio Carlucci, 10. enjoyed life on the farm but was a little lonely; He, 11. lived several miles away and rarely visited; friends, 12. had immigrated to the United States in 2008 and settled on this remote farm; parents, 13. had worked hard to learn English but were still embarrassed about their accents; They, 14. longed for his own car and daydreamed of ways to pay for it; Alfio, 15. talked with each other in the kitchen but kept their voices soft; Carluccis, 16. knew of Alfio's loneliness and planned to do something about it; They

page 31

1. country, 2. people, 3. pen pal, 4. guy, 5. student, son, 6. home, 7. friends, 8. choice, 9. dancing, choreography,

10. friends, 11. one, 12. friends, 13. person, 14. visitors, 15. experiences, 16. memories

page 32
1. aghast, 2. alive, 3. eerie, 4. different, 5. solid, 6. strange, 7. saline, barren, 8. unique, fascinating, 9. fearful, 10–12. Sentences will vary.

page 33
1. earns; money, 2. boards; boat, 3. screech; greeting, 4. scans; horizon, 5. mark; positions, 6. uses; paint, flags, 7. pulls; traps, 8. wave; claws, 9. slips; pegs, 10. drops; traps, buoys, 11. cooks; lobsters, 12. memorized; recipe, 13–15. Sentences will vary.

page 34
1. promised; lessons; me, 2. won; laugh; me, 3. offers; trivia; readers, 4. gave; surprise; people, 5. fed; chestnuts; horses, 6. told; story; class, 7. give; warnings; masters, 8–10. Sentences will vary.

page 35
1. the marriage of Anne Burras and John Laydon; The first wedding in America, the marriage of Anne Burras and John Laydon, took place in 1609. 2. the Electrical Exposition; The first wedding broadcast on radio took place at a fair, the Electrical Exposition, in 1922. 3. a city seven miles away; The wedding march was played by radio station KDKA in Pittsburgh, a city seven miles away. 4. a parachute ceremony; My favorite strange wedding, a parachute ceremony, took place in 1940. 5. a minister, a bride, a groom, and four musicians; no commas needed, 6. the tenth president; John Tyler, the tenth president, was the first to be married while he was president. 7. Letitia; His first wife, Letitia, had died while he held that office. 8. a ceremony in a hot-air balloon; A "balloon wedding," a ceremony in a hot-air balloon, was held in 1874 in Ohio. 9. site of an air show; The city of Houston, site of an air show, was the location of the first wedding in an airplane. 10–11. Sentences will vary.

page 36
1. phrase, 2. clause, 3. phrase, 4. phrase, 5. phrase, 6. phrase, 7. phrase, 8. clause, 9. infinitive, 10. gerund, 11. prepositional, 12. participial, 13. prepositional, 14. infinitive

page 37
1. paint; had been scraped; dependent, 2. you (understood); fill; independent, 3. they; continued; independent, 4. shoulders and backs; ached; dependent, 5. painting; was revealed; dependent, 6. work; was; independent, 7. independent, 8. dependent; Because, 9. dependent; before, 10. independent

page 38
1–9. Sentences will vary. 1. Since Plato was a famous philosopher, Aristotle decided to attend his school. 2. After Plato died, Aristotle opened his own school to continue Plato's teachings. 3. After an earthquake occurs, tidal waves begin to form. 4. Unless you find shelter, you will be in great danger. 5. Although the highest number on the Richter scale is a 9, no earthquake has ever been recorded at that level. 6. Because earthquakes can be so damaging, architects try to make their designs strong. 7. The Richter scale is useful because it measures the magnitude of an earthquake. 8. When Pasha growled and whined, Cassie knew something was wrong. 9. While he paced the living room floor, Pasha barked at Cassie.

page 39
1. NC, 2. C, 3. NC, 4. NC, 5. C, 6. C, 7. compound sentence, 8. compound subject, 9. compound predicate, 10. compound sentence, 11. compound sentence, 12. compound predicate

page 40
Answers may vary. 1. We can wait for the package, or we can leave without it. 2. I'm driving to the office in an hour, so I'll pick up the supplies on the way. 3. Up went the lottery jackpot; down went our hopes of winning. 4. Ava was ready, but her mother was not. 5. We should respect our privileges; otherwise, we might lose them. 6. Scott scrubbed hard for two hours; still, the walls were not ready to paint.

page 41
1. When Lena's family made vacation plans, 2. Because the Harrisons lived in Texas, 3. Before the plane landed, 4. since they retired, 5. where they had a great view, 6–9. Answers will vary. 6. After they built a mission and a fort, the Spanish founded San Francisco in 1776. 7. When the California Gold Rush began in 1848, San Francisco grew rapidly. 8. Although the great earthquake and fire of 1906 destroyed much of San Francisco, the city was quickly rebuilt. 9. While foggy weather is common in June and July, most people don't mind it.

page 42
1. independent: You can talk to me; you can talk to your older sister, dependent: whenever you have a problem, 2. independent: rain pelted down; we rushed back inside, dependent: As we left the restaurant, 3. independent: The library didn't have the book; she looked for it online, dependent: that Sara needed, 4. independent: the sky gets dark early; the days seem a lot shorter, dependent: Since daylight saving time ended, 5. independent: The girls took a walk; their mom gave them hot soup, dependent: even though the day was chilly; when they returned 6. CD-CX, 7. CD-CX, 8. NOT CD-CX, 9. NOT CD-CX, 10. CD-CX

page 43
Answers will vary.

page 44
1–5. Revised sentences may vary. 1. What I want to say is that; Starfish are fascinating creatures. 2. that have suction

power; A starfish has little feet tipped with powerful suction cups. **3.** which is very sensitive; At the end of each arm is a sensitive eyespot. **4.** In spite of the fact that; Although the eyespot cannot really see things, it can tell light from dark. **5.** some are bigger than others; Starfish come in a variety of colors, shapes, and sizes. **6.** that are written; for you to follow, **7.** The first thing you do is, **8.** which goes in a northerly direction, **9.** Continue driving for, **10.** approximately, **11.** as you drive along, **12.** sitting right there, **13.** Answers will vary. To get to Wilma's house, follow these directions: First get onto Highway 42 and take it to the Sun Drive exit. Turn left and follow Sun Drive north for four miles. Turn left at the stop sign. Follow the narrow dirt road for about 1.3 miles. Look on the left for a bright yellow ribbon tied to a tree. Wilma's house is the large white house beyond the tree.

page 45
1. My; Miguel, **2.** Las Muchachas; *La Bamba*, **3.** Rosanna; Spanish; English, **4.** Meyers, **5.** Cascade, Washington; Valentine's Day, **6.** The; Cascaders Glee Club, **7.** Ray Bradbury; Heron Lake, **8.** What; *Harry Potter*; *Goblet; Fire,* **9.** Francis; The Star-Spangled Banner, **10.** *Holes*; Texan; Louis Sachar, **11.** That; Newbery Medal, **12.** Straus; Giroux, **13–16.** Sentences will vary.

page 46
1. "The bravest people in the world are doctors," Rani said. **2.** She continued, "Indira, my stepsister, has been working in Calcutta since March." **3.** "Does she work at Mercy Major Hospital or at Calcutta General?" Ben asked. **4.** "Actually, Indira is a specialist in internal medicine at the clinic on Empire Street," answered Rani. **5.** "Indira once worked with Mother Theresa, the famous Albanian nun," Rani finished proudly. **6.** Silvas High School Science Fair; Thur.; Nov.; N. Canyon Blvd. **7.** Danton Water Festival; July; Brighton Dam; Lakeview, MN, **8.** Jeannette Duran; Antero St.; Markham, Ontario, **9.** Capt. C. J. Hatori; *Ocean Star*; P.O. Box; Gateway, NH

page 47
1. wishes, **2.** safes, **3.** taxes, **4.** heroes, **5.** peaches, **6.** kisses, **7.** keys, **8.** personalities, **9.** vacations, **10.** women, **11–13.** Sentences will vary. **11.** deer, **12.** handfuls, **13.** oxen,

page 48
1. A hummingbird's feet are so weak that the bird never walks. **2.** Hyraxes' feet form suction cups to climb trees. **3.** A sloth's feet are specialized for hanging in trees. **4.** Giraffes' forefeet are used for kicking predators. **5.** A centipede's body can have 95 pairs of legs. **6.** Pandas' paws have "thumbs" that help them grasp bamboo shoots. **7.** geese; geese's, **8.** wolves; wolves', **9.** spies; spies',

page 49
1. My favorite instrument, the trumpet, has a long history. **2.** Trumpets, in fact, are at least 3,500 years old. **3.** Silver and bronze trumpets were found in the tomb of Tutankhamen, the boy pharaoh of ancient Egypt. **4.** In the opinion of many experts, these trumpets were used for royal ceremonies. **5.** Originally, however, trumpets could sound only one or two notes. **6.** In very ancient times, bones and reeds were hollowed out to make trumpets. **7.** By 1400, though, the straight trumpet was bent into an S-shape. **8.** Later, I've read, it became a single-form loop. **9.** According to the encyclopedia, valves came into use only in the nineteenth century. **10.** I asked Mr. Ortega, our band leader, about the trumpet. **11.** "Mr. Ortega, when did you learn to play the trumpet?" **12.** "My uncle, a fine trumpet player, taught me when I was only ten years old." **13.** "Who are your favorite trumpeters, sir?" **14.** "Perry, the greatest masters of the trumpet include Louis Armstrong and Miles Davis." **15.** "You know, Perry, some jazz trumpeters also play classical music." **16.** "Wynton Marsalis, for example, is a fine classical musician."

page 50
1. The astronomer explained that a white dwarf is a tiny, dense star. **2.** The captain entered the cockpit, checked the instruments, and prepared for takeoff. **3.** The man's sunken, weathered face seemed to tell a story of hardship. **4.** I chose the gift, Micah wrapped it, and Jeremy gave it to Kelly. **5.** C, **6.** Bruce found an old, worn-out medicine bag in the barn. **7.** The neighbors searched behind the garages, in the bushes, and along the road. **8.** Their adventure began on a cold, drizzly September morning. **9.** Eleanor Roosevelt's courage, humanity, and service will always be remembered. **10.** We drove through the green, rolling hills of Pennsylvania. **11.** Buffalo Bill was a Pony Express rider, a scout, and a touring stunt performer. **12.** The hammer, the anvil, and the stirrup are parts of the human ear. **13.** C, **14.** I like Brandon because he is a warm-hearted, considerate person. **15.** Carla sneaked in and left a huge, beautiful, fragrant bouquet on the desk. **16.** Rufus can roll over, walk on his hind feet, and catch a tennis ball.

page 51
1. While human beings must study to become architects, some animals build amazing structures by instinct. **2.** The male gardener bower bird builds a complex structure, and then he decorates it to attract a mate. **3.** This bird constructs a dome-shaped garden in a small tree, and underneath the tree he lays a carpet of moss. **4.** After he covers the moss with brilliant flowers, he gathers twigs and arranges them in a circle around the display. **5.** Tailor ants, which might be called the ant world's high-rise workers, gather leaves and sew them around tree twigs to make their nests. **6.** These nests, which are built in tropical trees, may be one hundred feet or more above the ground. **7.** Adult tailor ants don't secrete the silk used to weave the leaves together, but they squeeze it from their larvae. **8.** After the female European water spider builds a waterproof nest under water, she

© Houghton Mifflin Harcourt Publishing Company

Answer Key
Core Skills Language Arts, Grade 7

stocks the nest with air bubbles. **9.** This air supply is very important, for it allows the spider to hunt underwater. **10.** The water spider lays her eggs in the waterproof nest, and they hatch there.

page 52
1. Caring for a pet is a big responsibility; it takes a lot of time and effort. **2.** My dog Homer is my best friend; however, I get angry with him occasionally. **3.** Homer is like all dogs; he be a pest sometimes. **4.** A cat fell from a boat into the lake; Homer jumped right in after it. **5.** Homer can be noisy, dirty, and disobedient; still, he is irresistible. **6–8.** Sentences will vary.

page 53
1. Animals need care in the following areas: shelter, food, exercise, and grooming. **2.** I am responsible for these chores: feeding the dog, walking him, and sweeping up the dog hair. **3.** I have to walk our dog, Homer, at 6:30 every morning. **4.** Sometimes Homer—watch out!—can be very destructive. **5.** Our previous dog, Cuthbert (1998–2012), was not nearly as accident-prone as Homer is. **6.** Of course, Cuthbert was a different kind of dog—about 80 pounds worth of different! **7.** Another curious thing—Homer is very fond of our vet.

page 54
1. In English class this year, we studied Lois Lowry's novel The Giver. **2.** In the library, Gil found a copy of Laurence Yep's book Dragon's Gate. **3.** Kara liked Langston Hughes's poem "Long Trip." **4.** Maria's favorite short story was "After Twenty Years" by O. Henry. **5.** The Story Machine is a play by Isaac Asimov. **6.** I like the magazine Newsweek. **7.** It's a Wonderful Life, **8.** "A Young Style for an Old Story", **9.** "Getting to Know You", **10.** "The Song of the Moon"

page 55
1. "Queen Elizabeth I ruled a great empire," said Marcia. **2.** She told her critics, "I have the heart and stomach of a king." **3.** "Who else had a great impact on a country?" asked Terri. **4.** "Well," Ben remarked, "Mohandas Gandhi inspired a nonviolent revolution in India." **5.** "Teach me how to play chess," said Devon. "What are these eight small pieces called?" he questioned. (new paragraph) "Those pieces," Sarah answered, "are called pawns. They are the weakest pieces on the chessboard." (new paragraph) "How about the queen?" asked Devon. (new paragraph) "Now the queen is a different story. She can move in any direction until her path is blocked," Sarah explained. (new paragraph) "So," Devon reasoned, "if your queen is captured, I guess you're in real trouble." (new paragraph) "Not necessarily," Sarah replied. "I've won games with only two bishops and a rook."

page 56
1. F, **2.** NM, **3.** 2.5 mL, **4.** Gov. Smith, **5.** NBA, **6.** mph,

7. CIA, **8.** Inc., **9.** September, **10.** feet, **11.** centimeters, **12.** Florida, **13.** Federal Bureau of Investigation; initialism, **14.** self-contained underwater breathing apparatus; acronym, **15.** United Nations; initialism, **16.** read-only memory; acronym

page 57
1. Aren't you the novelist who wrote this book? **2.** In my opinion, the photo on your book's jacket won't be any advantage to you. **3.** Why can't new novelists have some common sense? **4.** Perhaps you can take advice from someone who's got experience. **5.** You'll be sorry for putting a grinning photo on your book. **6.** I've got only one author photo on my shelf—this one of myself. **7.** didn't, **8.** won't, **9.** she's, **10.** who's, **11.** doesn't, **12.** she's

page 58
1. pre; ic; related to the time before recorded history, **2.** un; ant; inclined to feel no shame, **3.** de; ation; the act of taking forests away, **4.** co; ence; the act of living together

page 59
1. study of life, **2.** to make larger, **3.** act of speaking, **4.** able to be heard, **5.** to cause to be said, **6.** able to be removed or taken off, **7.** fighting against germs

page 60
CP: Homecoming, weekend, outstanding, classmates, grown-ups, hallways, forebears, ponytails, boyfriends, Meanwhile, baseball, basketball, afternoon, farewells; BL: brunch, glittered; CL: alums, Prep, dorms, chair; **1.** motel, **2.** splatter, **3.** flare, **4.** Internet, **5.** muppet, **6.** prissy, **7.** smog, **8.** fortnight, **9.** skylab, **10.** paratroops, **11.** dancercise, **12.** netiquette

page 61
Answers will vary. Possible answers: **1.** peculiar, **2.** produce, **3.** no one, **4.** inexpensive, **5.** artificial, **6.** lengthen, **7.** affect, **8.** unusual, **9.** workers, **10.** terrified, **11.** claimed, **12.** revolted, **13.** dangled, **14.** knowledge

page 62
Possible answers: **1.** depart; leave, **2.** energetic; peppy, **3.** horrid; disgusting, **4.** truth; trustworthiness, **5.** slowly; sluggishly, **6.** enemy; foe, **7.** interesting; exciting, **8.** display; show, **9.** calm; gentle, **10.** easy; simple, **11.** unfortunate; unlucky, **12.** retreat; withdraw, **13.** show; conceal, **14.** value; criticize; **15.** commander; follower, **16.** self-assured; uncertain, **17.** build; destroy, **18.** often; seldom, **19.** frightened; brave, **20.** purchase; sell

page 63
1. minute; very small; period of 60 seconds, **2.** content; everything contained inside something; satisfied, **3.** desert; arid land; abandon, **4.** lead; a metal; cause, **5.** wound; wrapped; injury, **6.** refuse; decline; garbage, **7.** dove; moved underneath; a pigeon, **8.** object; oppose; a material thing, **9.** stall, **10.** console, **11.** wind

page 64

1. tents; tense, **2.** where; wear, **3.** close; clothes, **4.** days; daze, **5.** air; so; need, **6.** rows, **7.** seems; our, **8.** knew; new; feet, **9.** not; scene, **10.** might; waist, **11.** piece, **12.** principal, **13.** border, **14.** build, **15.** paws, **16.** some, **17.** ball, **18.** hymn, **19.** alter, **20.** meat, **21.** site or cite, **22.** sent or scent, **23.** weigh, **24.** guest, **25.** eight, **26.** blue

page 65

1. b, **2.** c, **3.** d, **4.** a, **5.** bargain with someone, **6.** pronounce words clearly, **7.** bug that feeds off another animal, causing it harm

page 66

1. left; neutral, **2.** abandoned; negative, **3.** gaudy; negative, **4.** ornate; positive, **5.** paintings; neutral, **6.** masterpieces; positive, **7.** loud; negative, **8.** enthusiastic; positive

page 67

1–8. Sentences may vary. **1.** come across; For our English assignment, we are to list all the idioms we notice as we read. **2.** a piece of cake; Because I have spoken English for only three years, understanding idioms is hardly a simple task for me. **3.** come a long way; Nevertheless, I have improved in the past three years. **4.** best bet; Marta thinks works of modern fiction are the most likely place to find idioms. **5.** take my time; Because I need to make a good grade, I'm going to work carefully on the assignment. **6.** get the hang of it; Marta says I will do well if I concentrate on the exact meaning of each word. **7.** bend over backwards; Fortunately, my tutor is willing to make every effort to help me improve my English. **8.** In the long run; Eventually, studying idioms will help me to better understand my new language.

page 68

1–9. Sentences may vary. **1.** the bottom line; In business, profit is usually the primary goal. **2.** a ballpark figure; The cost of adding to the product line is an estimate. **3.** go out in a blaze of glory; Let's close the final year of the project with great fanfare. **4.** see the light of day; That strange new scooter design will never actually be produced. **5.** back to square one; The customer rejected the sketches, so the architects must start over. **6.** beyond a shadow of a doubt; These lottery numbers are undoubtedly the winners. **7.** grind to a halt; Production will stop if the rumored layoffs occur. **8.** state-of-the-art; The university's new computer system provides the most current technology. **9.** a definite no-no; Using nonstandard English is completely unacceptable.

page 69

1–10. Sentences will vary. **1.** S, **2.** M, **3.** S, **4.** S, **5.** M, **6.** M, **7.** S, **8.** S, **9.** M, **10.** S

page 70

1. hyperbole, **2.** hyperbole, **3.** allusion, **4.** allusion, **5.** hyperbole, **6.** hyperbole, **7.** allusion, **8.** allusion, **9.** allusion, **10.** hyperbole, **11–15.** Answers will vary.

page 71

1. are, **2.** is, **3.** give, **4.** is, **5.** deserves, **6.** understands, **7.** work, **8–15.** Answers will vary.

page 72

1. Hardly nobody; Hardly anybody knows about the mummy the Russians found in Siberia. **2.** hadn't barely; Gold prospectors had barely begun digging when they found something strange. **3.** No one, never, nothing; No one had ever seen anything like it. **4.** Nothing; correct, **5.** couldn't scarcely; Scientists could scarcely believe it—it was a baby mammoth! **6.** hadn't; correct, **7.** wasn't no; Although this mammoth was very young when it died, it wasn't a tiny creature. **8.** couldn't hardly; The prospectors could hardly get the mummy out of the ground.

page 73

1. ain't; Our people need good health care, and we aren't about to take no for an answer. **2.** knowed; The test wasn't as difficult as I expected, but nobody knew the answer to the bonus question. **3.** growed; "Why, look at those kids. They're all grown up!" said Great Aunt Matilda. **4.** throwed; At the last World Series, the President threw out the first ball. **5.** busted; Frank fell out of the tree and broke his arm. **6.** brung; The blind date should have been successful, but the guy brought along his dog! **7.** drawed; Raymond couldn't believe a 6-year-old drew the winning raffle ticket. **8.** heared; He heard the little girl's feet couldn't even touch the pedals. **9.** drownded; Hurricanes nearly drowned half of Louisiana this season. **10.** blowed; The gale-force winds blew at nearly 70 miles per hour.

page 74

1. him; Martin Van Buren, **2.** herself; Emma Edmonds, **3.** them; soldiers, **4.** they; soldiers, **5.** she; Julia Ward Howe, **6.** her, Howe, **7.** their; poets, **8.** who; soldiers, **9.** she, **10.** their, **11.** herself, **12.** she

page 75

Sentences may vary. **1.** A; Writers are inspired by cats. **2.** P; Mark Twain named his favorite cats Beelzebub, Blatherskit, Apollinaris, and Buffalo Bill. **3.** A; When Alice was in Wonderland, she was given orders by the Cheshire Cat. **4.** A; Dick Whittington was helped by a cat to become mayor of London. **5.** P; T.S. Eliot wrote the poem "A Naming of Cats." **6.** P; According to Rudyard Kipling, a cave woman first domesticated the cat. **7.** P; Most children enjoy books about cats. **8.** A; *The Cat in the Hat*, a book which has delighted young children since 1957, was written by Dr. Seuss.

page 76

1. in the cafeteria; In the cafeteria, we talked about the track meet. **2.** on the bottoms of its feet ; The lynx grows hairs on the bottoms of its feet for walking on snow. **3.** Made from matzo meal; Rachel shapes tasty dumplings made from matzo meal. **4.** who lives in Denver, Colorado; My friend

Tracy, who lives in Denver, Colorado, visited me.
5. Swinging wildly from branch to branch; I watched the chimpanzee swinging wildly from branch to branch. **6.** with chopsticks; Hoy taught us how to eat rice with chopsticks. **7.** Filled with daisies; The girls walked through the field filled with daisies. **8.** frequently; Annie frequently goes jogging in the park when she gets home.

page 77
Revised sentences will vary. **1.** When performing on stage, do not place the microphone too near the speaker cones. **2.** Standing near the runway, we found the noise of the jets deafening. **3.** Worried, Nick developed deep creases on his forehead. **4.** I found the missing baseball card when I was cleaning my closet. **5.** Tired from the long walk through the snow, they welcomed food and rest. **6.** Frightened, the rabbit perked up its ears and twitched its nose. **7.** To stay healthy and energetic, a person needs good nutrition. **8.** Mexico City was their home before they moved to Pittsburgh. **9.** Exploring the cave, the group discovered a new tunnel.

page 78
1. It was a bitter cold night for speed skating, but the three teams gave their all for the regional competition. Most surprising was the performance of Coolidge High, which outskated the other two teams in every category. They were the easy winners. **2.** Johnson raced down the court. He stopped dead, raised those incredibly long arms, and sunk the ball slow-motion into the basket. He scored 33 points before the final quarter ended. **3.** The third and fourth sentences shift to past tense because the writer has begun to describe the father's past. **4.** I had never seen a rodeo before. I expected the events to be tough and exciting. What I didn't expect was the gracefulness and incredible agility involved. I was glued to my seat.

page 79
1. sat, **2.** set, **3.** lay, **4.** sat, **5.** raised, **6.** lain, **7.** rise, **8.** laid, **9.** lies, **10.** Set, **11–14.** Sentences will vary.

page 80
1. b, **2.** b, **3.** a, **4–5.** Paragraphs will vary.

page 81
1. first-person point of view, **2.** author's use of the pronouns *my*, *me*, *I*, and *I'd*, **3. a.** ophthalmologist's exam, **b.** eye-hand exercises with optometrist, **c.** parents' continued encouragement and pride in writer's work, **d.** receipt of art books from grandmother, **e.** author's continued practice, **f.** author used imagination and developed own style, **4.** The writer will become a famous artist or cartoonist. **5.** Hard work and persistence pay off.; You can overcome odds if others believe in you.

page 82
Dialogues will vary.

page 83
Revised passages will vary.

page 84
Graphic organizers will vary.

page 85
Personal narratives will vary.

page 86
Checklist results will vary.

page 87
Errors are corrected in bold type.

   [paragraph indent] The first time **your** parents leave you at home alone is exciting for every child**,** I guess. In my case, however, there was a little more excitement than I had anticipated. I was fourteen, my sister Josie was ten, **Jeannie** was seven, **Kathryn** was six, and my brother Messy was just two. Mom and Dad were just going a few miles away to their favorite restaurant. It was their **anniversary**.

   "I'll just tuck Messy into his crib," Mom said. "He'll probably go right to sleep."

   [paragraph indent] "Just try to keep things quiet here," added Dad. "We'll be back in about three hours."

   [paragraph indent] I was "in charge," and I felt pretty grown-up about it. The Romeros**,** our next-door neighbors**,** had been **briefed** by my parents and were watching us **carefully**.

   [paragraph indent] That turned out to be a very good thing. My sisters and I were playing checkers when we heard a strange sound. It was a muffled roaring, and it seemed to get louder and louder. Luckily, the Romeros were soon banging on the door, and I was free to panic.

   [paragraph indent] "**Tornado!**" boomed Mr. Romero. We raced to our rooms, threw blankets over our pajamas, grabbed Messy, and dashed to the **Romeros'** basement.

page 88
1. jogging and rowing, **2.** equipment used; body parts exercised; advantages; disadvantages, **3.** How jogging and rowing are alike: Both provide aerobic exercise for the heart and lungs. Both have advantages and disadvantages. How jogging and rowing are different: Jogging uses very little special equipment, but rowing requires expensive machines. Jogging can be done outdoors, but rowing is done indoors. The disadvantages of jogging are possible damage to joints, accidents due to heavy traffic, and inhaling car fumes. The disadvantages of rowing are the expense, the boredom, and the repetitiveness.

page 89
1. relevant, **2.** irrelevant, **3.** relevant, **4.** relevant, **5.** irrelevant, **6.** irrelevant, **7.** relevant, **8.** relevant, **9–12.** Answers will vary.

page 90
Graphic organizers will vary.

page 91
Compare and contrast papers will vary.

137

page 92

Checklist results will vary.

page 93

Errors are corrected in bold type.

As people's awareness of animal rights has **grown,** so has the controversy over zoos. Collectors for zoos take animals away from their families and out **of** their natural habitats. They transport the animals long distances, often under difficult traveling conditions. Zoos are **confining,** and animals that are placed in them may be prevented from following **their** natural instincts. To supply the demand for wild creatures, poachers catch some animals **illegally.** Certain exotic animals are disappearing from the wild altogether, upsetting the balance of **nature.**

On the other hand, zoos increase people's awareness of the uniqueness and diversity of the animal population. Many people **didn't** begin to care about dolphins **[delete comma]** and dolphin safety until they had seen these beautiful, playful animals at zoos or theme parks. Many people now appreciate the importance of the rain forests because they have encountered **its** beautiful creatures. It **is** possible that zoo animals would be **[delete more]** happier in the wild. However, some natural habitats have disappeared so **completely** that, without the zoo population, many species would now be extinct. Perhaps we need zoos as a refuge.

page 94

1–3. Answers will vary.

page 95

1–19. Answers will vary.

page 96

Graphic organizers will vary.

page 97

Descriptive narratives will vary.

page 98

Checklist results will vary.

page 99

Errors are corrected in bold type.

I woke in the early morning. The **planet's** three suns, shining through the sides of the tent, created a strange orange glow in the air. It was bitterly cold. I lay in my down **[delete comma]** sleeping bag, watching my breath frost in front of my eyes. **There** was not a sound, not a stirring of wind, not a bird, not a crack of a twig. It was the kind of **quiet** that made me think of danger, and that was a thought I did not need on this still, freezing morning millions **of** miles from home.

I unfurled the stiff, gray cover to the little window in the side of the tent, which I could just reach from the sleeping bag. Outside was a landscape of snow and ice, blue and purple below the sky's dim glow. Heavy, straight growths, almost like tree trunks, stuck up out of the snow. None of them had any branches or twigs or, presumably, **leaves.** We

had not even determined **whether** they were living things.

A low, jagged mountain shimmered in the distance. Crystal **Mound** was **its** name. I knew it was formed of strange crystalline shapes of rose, turquoise, and yellow, though its colors looked washed out at this distance. I also **knew** that it was growing. We scientists had watched it grow. It was, **strangely** enough, the only thing on this silent planet that did seem to expand or change.

page 100

1. list of materials, **2.** introduction of subject, **3.** time-order words, **4.** correct order of sequence

page 101

Answers may vary. Step 1: Gather all the equipment you will need. Step 2: Mix detergent with warm water in a bucket. Step 3: Begin all work at the top of the car and work downward. Step 4: Wash the exterior of the car thoroughly. Step 5: Rinse all soapsuds completely using a garden hose. Step 6: Dry the car with a chamois. Step 7: Use window cleaner to clean the windows. Step 8: Vacuum the inside of the car.

page 102

Paragraphs will vary.

page 103

Graphic organizers will vary.

page 104

How-to papers will vary.

page 105

Checklist results will vary.

page 106

Errors are corrected in bold type.

As the holidays approach, do you dread all those **hours** you will spend **wrapping** gifts? Your worries may be over. Wrapping presents for your family and **friends** can be an enjoyable experience if you follow these simple rules. First, **buy** all your wrapping supplies early. Go to a well-stocked paper store and buy these items: gift wrap, ribbon, tape, tissue paper, and gift tags. Keep all your wrapping supplies together in one big bag. **Then** wrap as you go. Each time you buy a present, pull out your special bag and wrap the gift. When the **right** time comes, enjoy giving your beautifully wrapped presents.

Wrapping a package that contains **breakables** takes **patience** and the right wrapping materials. First, find a sturdy box a few inches larger than the object you are mailing. Then, buy plastic bubble wrap or foam "peanuts." **Surround** the object on all sides with padding and be sure it cannot move within the box. Then, use strong, **tough** tape to seal the box. Finally, be sure to write **FRAGILE** on the box in large, clear letters **[delete period]** so everyone who handles your package will know it contains something breakable.

page 107

1. High school football should be banned. **2.** the first paragraph, **3.** appeal to reason, appeal to emotions, **4.** Responses will vary.

page 108

Transitions and revised paragraphs will vary.

page 109

Graphic organizers will vary.

page 110

Opinion essays will vary.

page 111

Checklist results will vary.

page 112

Errors are corrected in bold type.

The people of the **world** are faced with alarming environmental problems. I am convinced that we must all cooperate through international **agencies** to solve these problems. Working alone, one state or **[delete unnecessary or]** one nation cannot protect its land and people from environmental **hazards**. The problems faced by people in the **United States** are also problems for people in **Canada**, Japan, and **Russia**. Only by facing these problems together and trying to work out cooperative solutions can we protect ourselves and our **planet**.

International cooperation is needed for several reasons. **In** the first place, some environmental dangers threaten the whole planet rather than local areas. Damage to the ozone layer is a good example. If someone in Nebraska uses an aerosol spray, the chemicals do not stay in Nebraska. Those damaging chemicals travel to the ozone layer, where they **affect** the **whole** world. Therefore, a **state** or **country** cannot protect itself against ozone damage simply by passing a law **forbidding** the local use of aerosols.

page 113

1. b., **2.** a., **3.** b., **4.** the first sentence, **5.** the first sentence, **1–5.** Explanations will vary.

page 114

Paragraphs will vary.

page 115

1. formal, **2.** formal, **3.** formal, **4.** informal, **5.** informal, **6.** informal, **1-6.** Rewritten sentences will vary.

page 116

1. fiction, **2.** reference, **3.** nonfiction, **4.** reference, **5.** periodical, **6.** reference, **7.** fiction, **8.** reference, **9.** nonfiction, **10.** reference, **11.** periodical, **12.** biography, **13.** fiction, **14.** reference, **15.** biography

page 117

1. glossary, **2.** bibliography, **3.** copyright page, **4.** title page, **5.** acknowledgments page, **6.** index, **7.** title page, **8.** Answers will vary; should include contents page

page 118

1. Chapter 4; These animals are mammals., **2.** Chapter 7; "Oceans in Danger" suggests pollution., **3.** Chapter 4, **4.** Chapter 2, **5.** Chapter 1, **6.** Glossary, **7.** Chapter 5, **8.** Chapter 3, **9.** Chapter 7, **10.** Chapter 6

page 119

1. 1, **2.** 68, **3.** no, **4.** Dip; Pickle and Relish; Spread, **5.** main food or ingredient, **6.** Acorn Squash, **7.** Almonds and Stuffed Celery, **8.** Flour, **9.** Appetizer(s)

page 120

1. noun, **2.** adjective, **3.** extending throughout or across a nation, **4.** nation, **5.** a tribe or federation, **6.** national, **7.** 3, **8.** yes

page 121

Sentences will vary. **1.** Henry's heart pounded as the ship pushed forward. **2.** The waves swelled while the ship turned toward the storm, as if to meet it head-on. **3.** Henry's first voyage as a working sailor was already more exhilarating than his wildest dreams. **4.** The black clouds loomed overhead, but the captain seemed to ignore them. **5.** The wind blasted against the sails and plunged the ship in and out of foaming white water. **6.** A cold chill reached Henry's skin from deep inside his stomach, as his excitement turned to terror. **7.** High up on the ship's bridge, the skilled captain looked down at the crew working on the deck. **8.** Noticing the look of fear on young Henry's face, the captain suddenly descended to the deck. **9.** He wanted to assure the crew that the storm would soon pass and the sea would become calm once again. **10.** But who can really soothe an inexperienced sailor who is about to encounter his first raging storm?

page 122

Answers may vary with reference. **1.** from the southeastern and south-central regions of the U.S. to Argentina, **2.** snails, earthworms, insects, and spiders, **3.** bony plates on their upper bodies; strong claws used to burrow into the ground, **4.** up to 15 pounds (6.8 kg), **5.** Hillary and his guide were the first two men to climb to the top of Mount Everest and return. **6.** New Zealand, **7.** as a beekeeper, **8.** 29,028 ft (8,848 m), **9.** southern Africa, **10.** no, **11.** Rhodesia, **12.** cattle, coffee, corn, cotton, sugar, tea, tobacco, wheat, **13.** It is an excellent source of carbohydrates, provides energy, contains B vitamins and minerals, and is easy to digest. **14.** in Asia, **15.** in fields covered with shallow water, **16.** in Asia

page 123

1. Nashville, **2.** nine; North Carolina, **3.** about 6,500,000 people, **4.** Great Smoky Mountains National Park, **5.** I-40, **6.** west, **7.** the Appalachian Mountains, **8.** Answers will vary depending on atlas used. **9.** central, **10.** yes; no body of water, **11.** Austria, France, Italy, Liechtenstein, Germany, **12.** the Rhine River and the Rhone River, **13.** Bern, **14.** the Alps, **15.** temperate, **16.** German, French, Italian, Romansch

page 124

1. Leonardo da Vinci, **2.** the United States; France, **3.** the Wright brothers; Blériot; Scott; Earhart; Lindbergh; Cochran, **4.** Andrée; Lindbergh; Cochran, **5.** the United States, **6.** Italy; Sweden, **7.** Earhart

page 125

1. almanac, encyclopedia, **2.** thesaurus, **3.** encyclopedia, **4.** dictionary, **5.** *Books in Print*

page 126

1. 700–799 (Arts and recreation) or 800–899 (Literature), **2.** 200–299 (Religion) or 300–399 (Social sciences), **3.** 400–499 (Linguistics/language), **4.** 600–699 (Technology), **5.** 000–099 (General reference) or 900–999 (General geography and history), **6.** none; The DDS does not include works of fiction. **7–10.** Answers will vary.

page 127

1. glaciers, because it is explained or defined, **2.** Waves, **3.** What is one reason that Cuban Americans have been successful?, **4.** Blood vessels, because that is what the paragraph is about

page 128

1. quickly but carefully, looking for the subject and the organization of the material, **2.** quickly but carefully, looking for key words and phrases, **3.** the encyclopedia entry about hogs, **4.** the story about Amanda and the homeless pig, **5.** slowly and carefully, paying attention to the part of speech and the definition, **6.** the encyclopedia entry about hogs; The notes may be needed to write a research report.

page 129

Notes should include key ideas. Suggested responses: Queen Hatshepsut: Only woman pharaoh. Succeeded Thutmose II about 1504 B.C. Ruled 21 years. Productive: Trade improved. Major building program. *cheng*: Meng T'ien, inventor, before 200 B.C. Musical instrument, zither family. Long, curved sound box. Strings stretch length of box. Frets help produce melody. Descendants of *cheng*: *tranh* (Vietnam); *koto* (Japan)

page 130

I. main topic, A. subtopic, **1.** detail, **2.** detail, B. subtopic, **1.** detail, **2.** detail, **3.** detail

II. The Yeti
    A. Where it lives
        1. In Asia
        2. In the Himalayas
    B. What it looks like
        1. Large ape or man
        2. Covered with hair

Outlines will vary.